Vorwort

Liebe Abiturientin, lieber Abiturient,

jetzt ist es also soweit – das Abitur steht an. Vielleicht ist der Gedanke daran bei einigen von Ihnen mit Unsicherheit und Anspannung verbunden.
Nervöse Mitschüler und Mitschülerinnen verstärken dieses Gefühl oftmals noch. Die Sorge ist aber unbegründet, wenn man gut vorbereitet ist und weiß, was auf einen zukommt!

Das vorliegende Methodenheft mit CD-ROM wird Ihnen helfen, sich im Abitur sicher zu fühlen und auch die Zeit davor ruhig und zielgerichtet für Ihre individuelle Vorbereitung im Unterricht und zu Hause zu nützen.

Der Aufbau dieses Hefts orientiert sich an den kommunikativen Kompetenzen und Anforderungsbereichen im Abitur und bietet Ihnen die Möglichkeit, grundlegende und weiterführende *Skills* einzuüben. So trainieren Sie etwa an einem Sachtext Lesestrategien, an einem Dramenauszug das Erkennen von Stilmitteln und anhand von *Listening texts* schulen Sie Ihr Hörverständnis. Kapitel zu besonderen sprachlichen Stolperfallen, *Mediation* und *Speaking* vervollständigen die Abiturvorbereitung.

Die verschiedenen Teile des Methodenhefts müssen weder chronologisch noch vollständig bearbeitet werden. Sie können sich die Dinge aussuchen, die für Ihren Lernfortschritt wichtig sind, und das, was Sie schon sicher beherrschen, nur ganz kurz behandeln oder weglassen. Zu sämtlichen Aufgaben des Arbeitshefts finden sich detaillierte Lösungshinweise auf der beiliegenden CD-ROM.

Dort haben wir auch Übungsklausuren zur Vorbereitung auf die Abiturprüfung für Sie zusammengestellt. Zu jedem Themenfeld liegen Prüfungen gemäß der aktuellen Aufgabenformate zu *Listening, Reading, Text comprehension* und *-analysis, Writing* und *Mediation* und ausführliche Lösungshinweise vor. Anhand der Übungsklausuren können Sie sich zielgerichtet auf die Abiturprüfung vorbereiten und Ihre Lösungen mit den Lösungshinweisen und Erwartungshorizonten vergleichen. Zudem finden Sie auf der CD-ROM die Audiodateien und Transkripte vor.

Wir wünschen Ihnen viel Erfolg bei Ihrem Abitur!

Ihr Oberstufen-Team

Symbolerklärung

✎ **Hier sind Sie aufgefordert, direkt in das Heft hineinzuschreiben.**

▤ Bitte schreiben Sie hier auf ein separates Blatt.

◎ Diese Texte befinden sich auf der CD-ROM.

Inhalt

Listening

Reading

A Reading skills

B Writing skills

C Closed and half-open tests

Text analysis

A Referring to a text

B Non-fictional texts

C Fictional texts

D Visual texts

E Audiovisual texts

Evaluation

Mediation

Speaking

Language workshop

Listening

1 Listening skills

Listening is a very important skill for successful communication. In face-to-face communication you listen so that you can reply. In an exam situation the communication will be one-sided, i.e. you do not have to reply. The extracts you will have to listen to are usually taken from radio programmes, speeches, interviews etc.

Tip !

Watch films in English with English subtitles. This will help you to hear the difference between the spelling of words and their pronunciations.

Listening exams can be stressful and you might assume that you cannot do very much to prepare for them. But this is not altogether true. Use every opportunity to listen to spoken English outside the classroom. Listen to songs, TV, films, the radio, podcasts etc., to anything you are interested in. Make sure you listen to speakers from different parts of the world. Here is some more advice that might help.

☑	**Pre-listening**
	Your test is about a topic that you know something about. Predict some of the information that might be presented.
	Read the tasks carefully, make sure you understand.
	Find out how many different voices you will hear. You might find information in the instructions. This will help you prepare.
	Always look for clues that help you predict (e.g. title of the audio). What vocabulary do you know about it?
	Use your common sense. If the questions and options have numbers, dates or key words say them to yourself to think about the way they sound.
	Make sure you are familiar with the types of tasks. If it is multiple choice, read all the options carefully and underline the key words.
☑	**While listening**
	The context might help you to think about what the speakers are saying.
	Keep calm. If you don't understand one of the key words, don't stop listening. You must continue listening to the next part.
	If you are expected to give short answers, write numbers for the questions. Just write notes next to the numbers while you are listening. Write down key words, use abbreviations (e.g. info instead of information) and don't worry about spelling.
☑	**After listening**
	If the options in the multiple choice are confusing, answer the question in your own words. Then look at the options again and decide which one is similar to your idea.
	Answer all the questions even if you have to guess. If there are 4 options you have a 25% chance to find the correct answer.
	Before handing in your answers you can check grammar, spelling and punctuation.

1 1.1 Latinos in the USA

Tip !

In the exam you will have between 30 seconds to 2 minutes to read through the task. You will hear the audio twice. After listening you will have between 30 seconds to 2 minutes to finalise your answers.

Listen to a clip from a radio broadcast of Crossing Continents, BBC Radio 4's award-winning foreign affairs documentary series. In this episode the journalist Claire Bolderson goes to Aurora, Illinois to interview both Latinos and white Americans.

a) *Before listening, look at the title of the programme and the introduction and predict the topic and thematic vocabulary. Make a mind map.*

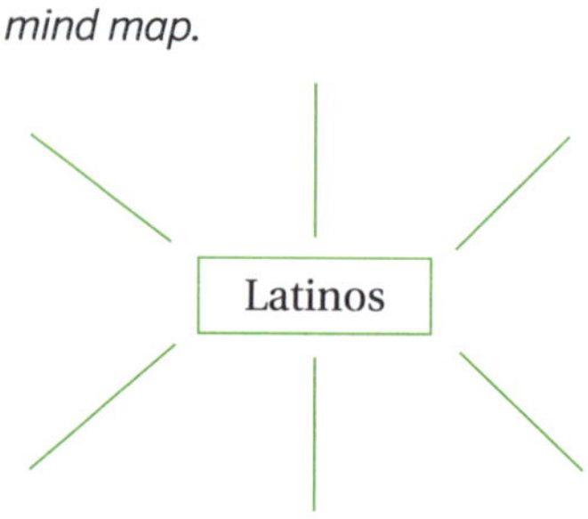

b) *Now listen to the audio. Match the statement and the speaker in the space provided below. There is one statement more than you need.*

1. Jerry Campaña
2. Clara Diaz
3. Tom Weissner
4. Claire Bolderson

A. Latinos display pride in their homes by maintaining a good appearance.
B. Latinos are extremely hard-working and willing to take the risks involved in self-employment.
C. The Latino population prevents the decline of city centres.
D. The main incentive for immigration is to provide better opportunities for the next generation.
E. Latinos find it particularly difficult to adapt to life in the small towns of the Midwest.

1. ______ 2. ______ 3. ______ 4. ______

c) *Complete the sentences with your own words.*

1. Claire Bolderson visits the small town of Aurora for her interviews because *(state two reasons)* ____

____

2. The Spanish name of a supermarket is an example of ________________________

3. Tom Weissner believes that the country's power ____________________________

d) *The programme is from 2012. Research current U.S. immigration policy and the Latino population's attitude towards it.*

2 1.2 Online shopping in India

You are going to listen to an excerpt from a radio programme about changing shopping habits in India. Mukti Jain Campion reports from the city of Bangalore.

Tip!
In the exam you will have between 30 seconds to 2 minutes to read through the task. You will hear the audio twice. After listening you will have between 30 seconds to 2 minutes to finalise your answers.

a) *Before listening to the audio, look at the title of the programme. It has got two parts. Jot down a few ideas about each part.*

Online shopping	in India
✎	✎

b) *What are your expectations concerning the speaker(s)?*

____

____

c) *What are the characteristics of Indian English?*

____

____

d) *Read the following text carefully before listening. Now listen to the audio and fill in the gaps. Don't be shocked if you find Bipin, the first interviewee, hard to understand.*

Tip!
It might be useful if you read the questions and options out loud to yourself to help you think about the way they sound.

Bipin, aged ______________, works as a motorbike courier in Bangalore. He shares a simple, ______________ home with a friend. Every morning he gets up at ______________, has a bath, says a ______________ and sets off to work.

e) *Tick the correct answer. In each item there is only one correct answer.*

1. What is Bipin's attitude to his job?
- [ ] a) He is dissatisfied with the pay.
- [ ] b) He dislikes the early starts.
- [ ] c) He enjoys meeting different people.
- [ ] d) He appreciates the responsibility.

2. Diwali, the Indian festival of light, is …
- [ ] a) a period of great buying activities.
- [ ] b) a season similar to Thanksgiving.
- [ ] c) a time of quiet worship.
- [ ] d) a difficult phase for selling goods.

3. Which of the following logistical problems does the reporter mention first?
- [ ] a) access to the Internet.
- [ ] b) availability of fast delivery.
- [ ] c) access to computers.
- [ ] d) availability of debit or credit cards.

4. The reliable delivery of goods depends on …
- [ ] a) the number of employees in logistics.
- [ ] b) the use of machines and computers.
- [ ] c) a combination of traditional labour and modern technology.
- [ ] d) the cooperation of the postal service and private companies.

5. Bipin is equipped with …
- [ ] a) a smartphone with GPS.
- [ ] b) safety clothing.
- [ ] c) a map of his delivery route.
- [ ] d) a safety deposit box.

3 1.3 Adieu EU

Tip!
In the exam you will have between 30 seconds to 2 minutes to read through the task. You will hear the audio twice. After listening you will have between 30 seconds to 2 minutes to finalise your answers.

After the referendum on leaving the EU, the former British Prime Minister David Cameron decided to resign. A few weeks of uncertainty followed. Eventually, Theresa May was elected to replace him. The speech you will hear was delivered outside 10 Downing Street.

a) *Tick the correct answer. In each item there is only one correct answer.*

1. At the opening of her speech Theresa May …
- [ ] a) praises her predecessor's achievements.
- [ ] b) pays tribute to the achievements of her party.
- [ ] c) promises to pursue a more modern course.
- [ ] d) paints a very pessimistic picture of the past.

2. According to Theresa May, David Cameron will be remembered …
- [ ] a) for his austerity measures.
- [ ] b) for campaigning against separatism.
- [ ] c) for his courage to break with traditions.
- [ ] d) for promoting communal fairness.

3. She promises to fight against discrimination …
- [ ] a) on the grounds of sexual orientation.
- [ ] b) on the grounds of race.
- [ ] c) on the grounds of age.
- [ ] d) on the grounds of religion.

4. According to Theresa May, working class families …
- [ ] a) can't afford to buy homes due to low incomes.
- [ ] b) spend a lot of money on their children's education.
- [ ] c) live in constant fear of losing their jobs.
- [ ] d) have low-paid, 9-to-5 jobs.

5. Theresa May dreams of …
- [ ] a) making Britain a world leader in social equality.
- [ ] b) creating a more just and inclusive society.
- [ ] c) strengthening the ties between the 4 parts of the UK.
- [ ] d) regaining independence from foreign influences.

b) *Match the living conditions/prospects (a–e) and the different social groups (1–6). Be careful. There is one more group than you need.*

a) low life expectancy
b) life in rented houses or flats
c) unfair financial treatment
d) little prospect of adequate support
e) excellent career opportunities

1. female workers/employees
2. poor people
3. people with a private school education
4. young people in general
5. second/ third-generation immigrants
6. people with psychiatric disorders

a) ______ b) ______ c) ______ d) ______ e) ______

4 1.4 An app to fall in love with

You are going to listen to an excerpt from a radio programme. In the first part the host Simon Maybin, interviews a New Yorker to find out how modern technology helps them find romance. In the second part, he interviews a sociologist.

Tip !
In the exam you will have between 30 seconds to 2 minutes to read through the task. You will hear the audio twice. After listening you will have between 30 seconds to 2 minutes to finalise your answers.

a) *Tick the correct box. There is only one correct solution.*

1. The reporter is meeting a woman …
- ☐ a) to go on a date with her.
- ☐ b) to learn about dating apps.
- ☐ c) to make sure she is safe.
- ☐ d) to act as her doctor.

2. The fact that the date has deleted his profile …
- ☐ a) came as a surprise to Whitney.
- ☐ b) is considered normal by Whitney.
- ☐ c) still disappoints Whitney.
- ☐ d) increased her curiosity.

3. Before the date the woman is …
- ☐ a) excited because it's her first date.
- ☐ b) frightened that the guy might not turn up.
- ☐ c) tired because she did not sleep enough the night before.
- ☐ d) anxious because of the reporter's ideas and questions.

4. The woman says she uses dating apps because …
- ☐ a) she is too lazy to go to parties.
- ☐ b) this is what young New Yorkers do.
- ☐ c) she likes using tools to help her cope with everyday life.
- ☐ d) she has got friends who met on a dating app, too.

b) *Fill in the missing information.*

Group	Age
people in the city, today	✎
women married today	✎
men married today	✎
people married middle of 20th century	✎

c) *Answer the question below.*

Describe the concept of emerging adulthood using two aspects mentioned in the clip.

____

____

____

____

Reading: A Reading skills

1 Reading skills

Tip !

Reading texts is an everyday activity which is more varied and more complex than we often think. In this chapter you will learn several reading skills which will help you to make the most out of the text in your *Abiturklausur*.

Depending on your purpose for reading and the amount of time you have, there are different reading techniques: **Extensive reading** means reading very fast, sometimes skipping sentences or parts of sentences. There are two basic reading techniques for this, which will both be useful in the exam situation: Skimming means reading only to get the gist, i.e. what the text is about, and scanning means looking for specific information. Both are explained in detail later.
Intensive reading, on the other hand, means reading word for word. In order to do well you are expected to understand what the text says directly as well as what is said between the lines.

In the exam situation you will need a combination of different reading skills:

- The first step should always be to look at the heading and subtitle, at the author, the source and the first few lines. Try to imagine what the text will be about (**anticipating**).
- After that, there is no clear order in which to proceed. In most cases, **skimming** is the next logical step to get a general idea of what the text is about.
- To get a detailed understanding of the whole text, **read** it **intensively**. Take notes and look up words which you don't understand and which are important for understanding the text. Sometimes it will be helpful to read the text more than once. If you want detailed information about just one aspect of the text, **scanning** is the best technique.

In this chapter you will find detailed explanations, examples and tasks for each reading skill. All of the exercises refer to a single text which is just about the same length and complexity as an exam text. This means that you can practise step by step how to get to grips with your English exam.

1.1 Getting started: Anticipating

Anticipating means **predicting** what you are going to read and what will come next. In other words, before you start reading you have certain **expectations** and while you are reading you constantly confirm or adapt them. This process leads to a deeper understanding of the text, and therefore is particularly important in the exam situation. Anticipating can be very tricky because how successful you are depends on how much you already know about the theme, the situation and the author.

To be able to predict what a text will be about, look at the following points. Of course not all of them apply in each case!

- the kind of text (**fictional**, e.g. an extract from a novel or drama, or **non-fictional**, e.g. a newspaper article, etc.)
- the **author** and his or her background
- the **time** and **situation** in which the text was written
- its **title**, **subtitle**, **lead** and **length**
- its **layout** and any **illustrations** belonging to it
- the **first few lines**
- the **tasks**, because they will show you what to focus on after getting the general idea

Once you have started to read, the things you have anticipated will help you to make sense of the text. It will be much easier for you to identify the underlying structure of the text or the connections between ideas – even if the text is very complex or you do not know all the words.

Now use your skills

To practise anticipating, look at the source, title, lead and the first paragraph of the text "Can familiarity build trust? …" and answer the following questions. As a start, several important phrases are already underlined in blue.

a) *Look at the source and the first line of the body of the text. What kind of information can you find in it about the author, the kind of text and the situation in which it was written?*

b) *Look at the title and the lead: Note down the possible topic of the article.*

c) *State the author's likely intention for writing this article.*

d) *What does the word 'familiarity' in the headline make you expect with regard to the whole article?*

Key:	underlined in blue = examples for 1.1 Anticipating
	underlined in red = examples for 1.2 Skimming
	underlined in green = example for 1.3 Scanning
	marked with yellow = words which are explained in 1.4 Dealing with unknown words (→ see p.11)

Can familiarity build trust? A white cop moves into black Atlanta neighborhood

One street in Atlanta shows why American race relations are so fraught – and the steps toward how they might be made whole.

Atlanta – Not long after Mike Costello moved into a renovated brick ranch on Ericson Street earlier this year, he was helping the cable guy at his house when shots rang out – first one, then another.

As a cop, Mr. Costello knew exactly what the pops were. And as a cop, he didn't just peer through the blinds. He ran outside. At first, he couldn't see anything amiss, but then Raymond Hinton came running fast around the corner.

Everyone on Ericson Street knew Ray. Wherever he was, trouble usually wasn't far behind. He'd had run-ins with the law before and usually hung with the wrong crowd. There was a felony on his record for getting caught with a rock of crack cocaine. And just as surely, everyone knew Costello was the new cop next door – even if, on that day, he was just in his street clothes.

In that moment, as the two men stood looking at each other in the echo of gunfire, the gears of America's debate on race clicked into place: The straight-laced cop and the troubled black man found in suspicious circumstances. The kaleidoscope of relations between police officers and the black community has often spun around just such scenarios. Whose suspicions were right? Whose actions were justified? Too often, those encounters have ended in death and national upheaval.

On this day, Mr. Hinton turned and ran.

When his fellow cops arrived on the scene, Costello told them what had happened, and they quickly zeroed in on Hinton as the guy who shattered the silence. But the thing was, Hinton was the victim. He was the one shot. He was the one doctors were able to save, but only barely.

The story of Atlanta's Ericson Street, in many ways, is a picture of why America remains so racially divided – but also of how it might be able to overcome that and put itself together.

The story of Officer Costello and Raymond Hinton didn't end amid recrimination and distrust, because the story of Officer Costello and Raymond Hinton still has not ended. They live right across the street from each other, after all.

Costello and other neighbors bought Hinton pizza and drinks to wish him well. It might seem a small thing, but to Hinton, it matters. The road to racial understanding, it turns out, can be a lot easier when you know whom you're looking in the eye.

Costello, white cop moved into black neighbourhood

Shooting in the new neighbourhood

Costello stops a black man

neighbours, know each other

support each other, even small things matter

"Don't get me wrong, Officer Costello is a good guy," Hinton says. "I mean, he's never said he's sorry or anything like that for pegging me as the shooter, and that's OK, I get it. But that's why I think it's good for cops to live where they work: It can take a while for people of different ethnicities to figure each other out, you know, but that doesn't mean you don't try to do it. I think it's really the one way we can bring it to understanding."

Costello is among a growing number of Atlanta officers moving into the neighborhoods they often patrol. For the 2015 Atlanta "Officer of the Year," home is now Edgewood, a blighted-but-improving neighborhood three miles from downtown. Many of Costello's neighbors are black, and one Edgewood resident runs a police watchdog group that once exhorted residents to throw bricks at police cruisers. Some did.

Many days Costello jogs by the spot where one of his friends was shot in the face and leg with a shotgun in an ambush three years ago. The friend recovered but gave up the badge.

Atlanta police hope that officers like Costello will help heal relations between the police department and the black community. Only 13 percent of the city's white cops live in the city. Critics counter that nothing but better training will make a difference.

Regardless of what it does for the Atlanta Police Department, however, Costello's move has changed him and those around him. For each, the change has been different and often subtle – the neighbor who resented police for how they pulled him over, the neighbor who was herself afraid to move to Edgewood, and the neighbor whose first instinct when he was shot was to flee from the police.

Frankly, Costello didn't have any idea how things would go when he decided to move to Edgewood.

He had lived in New York City, where he "knew all kinds of different people." His partner on the beat is black – a former stand-up comedian. And Costello was officer of the year for single-handedly collaring an armed home invader whose gun had already been fired.

But before he joined the Secure Neighborhoods Initiative, which gives cops a $300-a-month stipend to move into blighted neighborhoods, Costello he had never really spent a night in a neighborhood like Edgewood, where even the clergy are armed. In Atlanta, he had lived in Buckhead and Virginia Highlands, playgrounds of the Atlanta elite.

The Atlanta Police Department opted against a low-key arrival. The city rolled out a red carpet and news cameras showed up when Costello moved in. When they left, he took stock, started building a shed in the backyard, and hoped for the best.

"The cat was out of the bag," he says. "It would either turn out great, or it would be mayhem."

By Patrik Jonsson, from Christian Science Monitor, 28th September 2016

11 **felony** a serious crime • 22 **to shatter** to break/disrupt • 41 **to exhort sb** to strongly encourage sb., persuade sb. • 44 **badge** a piece of metal on your clothes that shows your rank or position in an organisation • 50 **to pull sb over** to stop sb's vehicle • 57 **to collar sb** to catch and hold sb • 60 **clergy** religious leader e.g. a priest • 62 **low-key** *(informal)* quiet, with hardly any excitement • 63 **to take stock** to get an overview of the situation • **source The Christian Science Monitor** reputable news organisation from the US

Tip !

In your exam, **note-taking** allows you to keep information for later use and to reorganise it for a particular task, e.g. writing a summary or characterising a person. Your notes should be short and clear. They should extract the main aspects or ideas and refer to the structure of the text.

1.2 Skimming through a text

Skimming is a useful technique whenever you want to quickly know what a text is about, for example when you have to decide quickly between two texts in your exam. When you skim through a text, you always try to look at whole sentences or paragraphs instead of reading word for word. You only read through the text quickly to get the gist, that is its **general idea**, **tone** and the **intention** of the author. This means

- identifying the **keywords** or **key sentences** for each passage of a text.
- recognising **important information** and distinguishing it from supporting details such as examples.

It can involve **underlining** or otherwise **marking** words or sentences in the text and can lead to **note-taking**, for example giving titles to the paragraphs or passages of a text. In this way skimming is a useful way to prepare for writing a summary.

Now use your skills

a) *In the first four paragraphs the main points/keywords and key sentences are underlined in red. Practise working through the rest of the text in the same way.*

b) *Take notes in the margin to prepare a summary. You can already find examples for such notes next to the text.*

1.3 Scanning a text

Scanning means **extracting specific information** from a text. You read selectively, only looking for the information relevant to your purpose. In most cases, this purpose is determined by a particular task in your exam, for example to describe, analyse or examine a particular aspect or to characterise a person in the text. As with skimming, you also mark the important information, e.g. by underlining with a new colour.

Now use your skills

a) *A typical task in your* Abitur *could be the following one:* ***Explain what is necessary to overcome racial violence between black people and the police according to the text.***
Look at the title and lead again and note down clues for your answer. (→ see p.8, Anticipating)

____

____

____

b) *Scan the text for all the information relevant to the task above and underline it. The first two important phrases are already underlined in green as an example.*

c) *Take notes in the margin. They can help you to write the answer to the task later on. There are already two examples for such notes next to the text.*

1.4 Dealing with unknown words

Intensive reading normally means that you try to understand all the words. In those cases where you are not allowed to use an English-German dictionary but only a monolingual dictionary, it is helpful to rely on **educated guessing** as a technique to deal with unknown words. This can save a lot of time even if you do have an English-German dictionary. Educated guessing means that you find out the meaning of unfamiliar words and expressions

- by finding **clues in the context**:
  Example: "The first rainfalls after an unusually long dry season will help to *mitigate* the hunger in this region." Even if 'to mitigate' is completely unfamiliar, you can guess that it means something like 'to reduce' because the situation for growing food has definitely improved with the rain.
- from **word families** and understanding **word formation**:
  Example: The word 'interracial' is perhaps unknown to you, but you probably know 'inter-' as a prefix meaning 'between', and you know the noun 'race' and that nouns can be turned into adjectives by suffixes such as '-ial'. With this in mind it is easy to understand terms such as 'interracial marriage'.
- from **similarities** between the English expression and German, or perhaps French and Latin:
  Example: English 'landscape' and German *'Landschaft'* have the same meaning and are very similar in writing. As another example, consider English 'to descend', French *'descendre'* and Latin *'descendere'*, which all mean the same ('going down').

Tip!
To understand the context it is also very important to pay special attention to linking words. Linking words help to structure a text by expressing logical relations between sentences, paragraphs and the ideas expressed in them. Understanding these relations correctly enables you to understand a text without knowing all the words.

Tip!
Never forget that some of these similar words are false friends, which only look the same but have a slightly or even completely different meaning!
(→ see p.107, Exercise 2)

Now use your skills

In the text, the author uses a couple of words which you may be unfamiliar with. Some of them are given in the annotations below the text, some others you can figure out yourself by educated guessing.

a) *Here you are given two paraphrases for each unfamiliar word or phrase. Tick the correct or more appropriate meaning and write an example sentence into the line below using the word.*

"pops" (l.6): ☐ police officers or: ☐ sounds of a shooting gun

____

"amiss" (l.7): ☐ strange, out of place or: ☐ missing, stolen

____

"run-ins" (l.10): ☐ meetings/appointments <u>or:</u> ☐ collisions, trouble

---

"straight-laced" (l.15): ☐ showing strict moral attitudes <u>or:</u> ☐ knocked down

---

b) *Fill in the blanks in the table below. Your way of guessing the right meaning can be different from the model solutions.*

Unknown word	Meaning/synonym/paraphrase	Method
kaleidoscope (l.16)	✎	Similarities: German 'Kaleidoskop' and French 'caléidoscope'
zeroed in (l.22)	✎	Context: Hinton is obviously a suspect. It is likely that the police officers will charge him for the shooting and that 'zero-in' means something in this direction. Word formation: 'zero' is part of the word and resembles a circle with which you can target sth.
on the beat (l.56)	on patrol/at work	✎
subtle (l.50)	quiet, hardly noticeable, fine	✎

c) *Look up the words in a dictionary and fill in the following table.*

Unknown word	Meaning/synonym/paraphrase	type(s) of word	**Further information** (word family, AmE/BrE, formal/informal etc.)
fraught (lead)	✎	adjective	AmE and BrE, formal
peg (l.34)	✎	✎	✎
blighted (l.39)	✎	✎	✎
mayhem (l.66)	✎	✎	✎

1 Writing skills

With the help of these reading skills, it is much easier for you to find the answers to the tasks. However, writing correct answers is not always easy. The following basic tips can help you to turn your ideas and notes into a well-structured and understandable text.

1.1 Getting started: Answering a comprehension question

There is no general rule for **answering comprehension questions**. However, the following guidelines can be helpful:

- If the task refers to the text, **scan** the text for points you want to use, **take notes** and order them.
- For an **introductory sentence** it can be useful to refer to the information given in the task.
- Sometimes it is unavoidable to use the words from the text but you should try to use **your own words** as much as possible.
- Use **linking words** to show the logical development of different points, ideas or arguments of your answer. (→ see the *Useful phrases* on p.72 and p.75)
- If your text is longer, divide it into **paragraphs**. (→ see p.73)
- Find a sentence that **concludes** your answer and has the form of a general statement.

Now use your skills

Again look at the task which you were given in the section on scanning: ***Explain what is necessary to overcome racial violence between black people and the police according to the text.***

This time, answer the task in a few paragraphs with the help of your notes from scanning the text. Write your answer, which should be about 150 words, on a separate sheet of paper and follow the hints for answering comprehension questions. Here is an example for the beginning, which is based on the notes already given in the margin of the text:

"Patrik Jonsson's example of Mr. Costello shows that it is essential for police officers to be familiar with the neighbourhood which they are responsible for. For this reason, Mr. Costello moved into the area he works in. It is also important to help each other. For example, ..."

1.2 Summary writing

Writing a good **summary** can be very difficult and tricky, particularly if the text you have to summarise is full of hidden and indirectly expressed meanings. Here are some basic rules to be remembered:

- At the beginning state the name of the author, the text type, title and main idea or topic.
- Use your own words as much as possible.
- Focus on the topical ideas or aspects and leave out any information that is not essential (e.g. examples, descriptive details etc.).
- Leave out quotations from the text and direct speech.
- Leave out your own interpretations and opinions.
- Use the present tense.

Tip!
To avoid using words from the text, paraphrase or explain words and use synonyms.

A summary should be **short** and give an **adequate and correct account** of what a text is about. How short is short? – A difficult question, but as a rule of thumb for your *Abiturklausur* if the text is about 800 words long, your summary should have between 150 and 250 words.
Check and if necessary revise your summary by putting yourself in the position of a reader who does not know anything about the text and its theme.

Now use your skills

Summarise Patrik Jonsson's article and pay attention to the hints given above. Work with your notes from skimming.

Your summary may start like this, for example:

"In his newspaper article "Can familiarity build trust? A white cop moves into black Atlanta neighborhood" from the Christian Science Monitor, Patrik Jonsson portrays a white police officer who moved into an Afro-American community. ..."

1 Closed and half-open tests

Reading tests seem easy to solve but they can be very tricky and you really have to concentrate. Some examples of common question types are:

- multiple choice questions (e.g. 3.2 Task a))
- true/false/(not in the text)/ questions (e.g. 3.2 Task d))
- sentence or table completion (e.g. 3.2 Task b), c))
- sequencing *(Anordnung in logischer Reihenfolge)*
- matching (e.g. 3.2 Task f))
- short answers *(Kurzantworten)*
- gap texts (e.g. 3.2 Task e))

To solve the reading tests, you have to apply the reading strategies and techniques of chapter 1 (Reading skills) here as well. For example, intensive reading is essential to get all the details of the text and to gain the most points possible in your exam.

1.1 Getting started: Anticipating

Tip !

In your exam, note-taking is important for recording what you have found out from the text. It allows you to keep information for later use and to reorganise it for a particular task.

To get a first idea of the topic and of the intention of the text, focus on the title, the introduction, subtitles, the source and the genre of the text. For example the title can tell you about the topic the text deals with. The source may reveal useful information about the author, the date of writing and the genre of the text. In this way you can anticipate important information about the text which supports your understanding. Then read thoroughly through the complete text.

Now use your skills

Look at the text and anticipate important information. Then read the text and take notes or mark important statements.

The psychology of phishing: why do we fall for terrible email scams?

Maybe your bank wants you to update your password; maybe a new Facebook friend wants to show you a funny web page. Maybe a Nigerian lawyer wants to pass on a legacy from a long-lost relative.

What all of these people are really after, of course, are your password, bank details and, ultimately money. Such phishing scams, says Microsoft, are costing the world as much as $5bn a year. For some reason, the UK is a favourite hunting ground for the phishers: here, says security firm Proofpoint, unsolicited email is almost three times more likely to contain a malicious link than in the US.

But who falls for these scams? Well, you do. While it's easy to assume that only the technologically illiterate will be vulnerable, new research shows that in fact the reverse is true.

A team of US scientists recruited a group of 150 students at the University at Buffalo and surveyed them about their online activity. Six weeks later, each received a Facebook friend request from a stranger. Those who accepted – and this was most of them – was then sent a message designed to mimic a phishing attack, grammatical errors and all.

It read:

"I got internship from my friend and she's looking for more people urgently!!! If you are interested to intern and would like more details, please reply with you Student ID No., UB Email User name, Date of Birth (dd/mm/yy) within the next three days."

The team found that the more regularly the students used Facebook, the more likely they were to fall for the phishing scam and give away their personal information, thanks to a mixture of complacency and a desire to please.

"Perhaps being connected to a large number of people makes it difficult to discern a friend from a stranger; or frequently interacting with the platform makes individuals more likely to overlook the nuances in the message that might reveal deception," the authors write.

"Hence, habitual Facebook users appear significantly more likely to be inattentive and automatically provide the information requested by a phisher."

Other studies have shown that women are more susceptible to phishing scams than men, as are people between 18 and 25 – this latter presumably explained by the same complacency that the Buffalo researchers revealed.

In terms of the scams themselves, the more urgent the message appears, the more likely people are to fall for it. And, earlier this year, Proofpoint researchers established the most effective email subject lines for phishers, and found that invitations to connect on LinkedIn came top – they were twice as likely to get the victim clicking as any other scam email. The fraudsters read these research reports too, which is why "Invitation to connect on LinkedIn" is now the most widely-used subject line in phishing scams.

But why are so many phishing emails so deeply implausible? One currently doing the rounds, for example, purports to come from Janet Yellen, the recently appointed chair of the US Federal Reserve Bank. Quite an important woman, then – so, surely, suspicions would be aroused when she writes: "I have your file here in my office and it says that you are yet to receive your fund valued at $850,000". Many are even more unlikely, littered with spelling and grammatical errors.

The answer is that the implausibility is a useful tool for the scammers. An entirely believable email would get millions of people falling for the bait – most of whom would catch on later when the scammers started requesting private banking details. This way, the fraudsters can avoid wasting their time on no-hopers, knowing that any replies they do receive are from people at the more naive end of the spectrum. As Microsoft researcher Cormac Herley has pointed out: "Since gullibility is unobservable, the best strategy is to get those who possess this quality to self-identify."

There's little to be done to stop the scammers – they're scattered around the world and good at evasion – but some people are at least having fun trying.

A group called "419eater", named for the section of the Nigerian penal code that deals with fraud schemes, serves as a forum for tips on scamming the scammers themselves. Members invent their own banks – Plunder & Flee Incorporated is a favourite – and even go so far as to set up meetings overseas, mocking up fake flight booking documents and demanding that the scammer book them a four-star hotel room.

"For the most part these criminals are not 'poor people trying to scratch a living', but are indeed very prosperous compared to their law-abiding countrymen, and many operate in highly organised, and highly successful criminal gangs," says the site's creator – who naturally prefers to remain anonymous.

"Millions of dollars are stolen on a daily basis, with absolutely no thought given to victims, who are losing vast amounts of money, homes, relatives, jobs and worse. Contrary to popular belief, it is not just 'greedy and stupid people' that fall for these scams."

Emma Woollacott, The New Statesman, 2014.

title **phishing** a method used by criminals to access personal data like passwords etc. • title **email scam** an illegal trick, crime or fraud • 34 **fraud** criminal activity to gain money by deceiving people

1.2 Working on the questions

After reading the text for the first time, read through the questions. Basically the questions ask for three kinds of information. In an exam you are expected to understand and present:

- the main ideas of the text
- specific information or details
- implicit information (i.e. the author's attitude, the atmosphere of the text, the setting of the plot etc.)

Most of the questions follow the chronological order of the information as presented in the text.

Often you have to support your answer with evidence from the text. To prove your answer, mark the corresponding lines or words in the text as soon as you have found them. In this way you can always find the relevant quotation quickly in the text at a later point of time. To refer to the text, always give the line(s) and note down the first and last three words of the quotation (example: l.1/ ll.1–3, "In the morning ... at the station"). If the quotation is shorter than six words, note it down completely.

Now use your skills

a) *Tick the correct statement. Use a quotation from the text to support your answer (line number(s) + the first and last three words).*

1. Most likely to fall for email scams are ...

☐ a) senior citizens.
☐ b) children.
☐ c) users of social networks.
☐ d) analphabets.

line(s):

Tip!
In multiple choice read the information provided in the stem (=first part) of the sentence carefully. Then look for the corresponding information in the text.

2. In contrast to the US, internet users in the UK are more likely to …

☐ a) be employed by Microsoft.
☐ b) find friends online.
☐ c) receive dangerous software.
☐ d) receive job offers online.

line(s): ______

3. The participants of a study of the University at Buffalo …

☐ a) created a mock phishing email.
☐ b) sent a phishing email to friends.
☐ c) reported the number of phishing emails in their mailbox.
☐ d) were contacted via Facebook.

line(s): ______

b) *Complete the table. Note down the content of the phishing email that was used in the University at Buffalo experiment.*

1. Person looking for help as mentioned in the email	✎
2. Content	✎
3. Information asked for	✎

Tip!
Use your own words to complete the sentence.

c) *Complete the sentence.*

According to research done by the University at Buffalo, people fall for email fraud because

(give two reasons) ______

______.

Tip!
Always give a quote from the text to support your answer. Otherwise you won't get any credits.

d) *Tick the correct answer. Use a quotation from the text to support your answer (line number(s) + the first and last three words).*

1. Criminals behind scam emails study research papers by computer scientists.

☐ True ☐ False

line(s): ______

2. The senders of fraud emails take care to write logical and trustworthy emails.

☐ True ☐ False

line(s): ______

e) *Complete the sentence.*

The author's attitude to the group '491eater' ______

because ______.

Tip!
Don't forget to fill in your solutions in the box!

f) *Match the organisations (1.–2.) and the descriptions (a)–d)) and note down your solutions in the box! There are two more descriptions than you need.*

1. Proofpoint	
2. Plunder & Flee Incorporated	

a) IT-company	
b) online travel agent	
c) an invented financial institution	
d) a London based IT-law firm	

Solution:	
1.	2.

Text analysis: A Referring to a text

1 Using quotations

When analysing a text it is important to prove that you can support your arguments with examples or aspects from the text. You can do this by including **direct** and **indirect** citations. Use the following abbreviations:

Abbreviation	stands for	used
p.	page	when referring to one page only (singular)
pp.	pages	when referring to two or more pages (plural)
l.	line	when referring to one line only (singular)
ll.	lines	when referring to two or more lines (plural)
f.	and the following	for page or line (singular)
ff.	and the following	for pages or lines (plural) → not stating the end of the reference
cf.	from Latin "confer"	for indirect citations; meaning "compare"
/	the end of a verse in a poem	when indicating the end of one verse and the beginning of the next

Here is an example of a sentence from an analysis dealing with the text "The psychology of phishing: why do we fall for terrible email scams?" on pages 14-15: *Emma Woollacott states in her article that certain groups of people are more likely to fall for phishers than others, such as frequent users of Facebook (**cf. ll.19-21**), females rather than males (**cf. l. 27**) and "people between 18 and 25" (**l. 28**).*

Have a closer look at the example sentence by focusing on the following quotations:

quotes in the analysis	original text (see page 14–15)	explanation
frequent users of Facebook (cf. ll. 25-26)	Hence, habitual Facebook users appear significantly more likely to be inattentive and automatically provide the information requested by a phisher.	indirect quote (use of compare)
females rather than males (cf. l. 27)	Other studies have shown that women are more susceptible to phishing scams than men, …	indirect quote (use of compare)
"people between 18 and 25" (l. 28)	… as are people between 18 and 25 …	direct quote (use of quotation marks)

Helpful tips:

- If you have got only one text to work with, you do not need to include **page** references because the numbered lines run through. If the line reference can be misunderstood, you should also include the page, e.g. (*cf.* ***p. 15, ll.1-2***).
- Be precise and state the exact line(s) when quoting – you can also use **and the following**, which is considered less exact.
- You can shorten, adapt or add to a quote by using ellipsis points in square brackets **[…]** → *The author warns: "**[T]he** more urgent the message appears, the more likely people are to fall for it." (l.30-31); Woollacott describes the used procedure: "Those who accepted […] was then sent a message designed to mimic a phishing attack, grammatical errors and all." (ll.13-14).*
- **Quotation marks** must be used for a direct quote and be aware of the position of the first mark compared to the German use – this is a common mistake.
- When quoting **direct speech** use '…' within your pair of quotation marks.
- The indirect quote, i.e. paraphrasing information in your own words, must always be marked with **cf.**!
- Mind the amount of quotations used in your analysis – your essay mostly needs to consist of *your* words.

Now use your skills

Fill in the gaps using the correct punctuation, abbreviations and line references. Refer to the text on pages 14 and 15.

The journalist Emma Woollacott writes in her article that the high costs of phishing fraud are an estimated _____ $5bn a year. _____ (________). She also refers to a secondary source which claims: _____ _____ he UK is a favourite hunting ground for the phishers: _____ unsolicited email is almost three times more likely to contain a malicious link than in the US. _____ (________). But apart from looking at countries and certain groups of people who are most likely to be affected by phishing, the author also investigates successful phishing methods. Woollacott lists the relevance of email urgency and argues that people are easily tricked if the given time frame is fairly short (________). Furthermore, experts found that particular email subject lines can be very harmful (________), leading to rather tragic results: _____ The fraudsters read these research reports too, which is why _____ Invitation to connect on LinkedIn _____ is now the most widely-used subject line in phishing scams. _____ (________).

Text analysis: B Non-fictional texts

1 Non-fictional texts: Speech

You listen to, read and produce non-fictional texts every day. You classify them according to their functions:

to instruct	how to use your new mobile, a recipe in a cookery book, the book you are using to improve your language skills …
to persuade	advertisement, speech during an election campaign, editorial …
to inform	newspaper article, scientific research paper, travel guide …
to entertain	feature article in a magazine, columns on general topics in newspapers, report about an interesting journey …

In this chapter, you will analyse three non-fictional texts:
- first a speech by Barack Obama
- second a newspaper article
- third a film review on *The Lord of the Rings*.

1.1 Getting started: The nature of speeches

In contrast to written texts – where the author does not face his readership and their reaction – a speech usually brings the speaker and his audience into immediate contact (except for speeches broadcast on radio or TV). To choose the appropriate subject matter, tone and wording of a speech, the speaker must consider the following aspects:

a) *Look at the chart below and fill in the gaps with your own examples.*

Aspects	Example
context of the situation	• e.g. the American President's State of the Union speech • e.g. after-dinner speech ✎
✎	• e.g. expert at a conference of scientists explaining ethical problems • e.g. politician in parliament or in election campaigns presenting his party's agenda
audience	• e.g. experts at an opening conference ✎

Now use your skills

b) *Read the speech on the following page and fill in the chart below with the information you get from the text.*

speaker	Barack Obama
role of speaker	President of the United States of America
audience	✎
occasion	✎

The following text contains excerpts from President Obama's farewell address, delivered in 2017. Barack Obama was president of the United States from 2009 until 2017. Having served the maximum of two terms in office, he was not allowed to run for office anymore and gave his farewell address on January 10, 2017, in Chicago, the city where he once started his career working with local communities.

President Obama's Farewell Address

THE PRESIDENT: Hello, Chicago! (Applause.) It's good to be home! (Applause.) Thank you, everybody. Thank you. (Applause.) Thank you so much. Thank you. (Applause.) All right, everybody sit down. (Applause.) We're on live TV here. I've got to move. (Applause.) You can tell that I'm a lame duck because nobody is following instructions. (Laughter.) Everybody have a seat. (Applause.)

My fellow Americans – (applause) – Michelle and I have been so touched by all the well wishes that we've received over the past few weeks. But tonight, it's my turn to say thanks. (Applause.) Whether we have seen eye-to-eye or rarely agreed at all, my conversations with you, the American people, in living rooms and in schools, at farms, on factory floors, at diners and on distant military outposts – those conversations are what have kept me honest, and kept me inspired, and kept me going. And every day, I have learned from you. You made me a better President, and you made me a better man. (Applause.)

So I first came to Chicago when I was in my early 20s. And I was still trying to figure out who I was, still searching for a purpose in my life. And it was a neighborhood not far from here where I began working with church groups in the shadows of closed steel mills. It was on these streets where I witnessed the power of faith, and the quiet dignity of working people in the face of struggle and loss. [...] This is where I learned that change only happens when ordinary people get involved and they get engaged, and they come together to demand it.

After eight years as your President, I still believe that. And it's not just my belief. It's the beating heart of our American idea – our bold experiment in self-government. It's the conviction that we are all created equal, endowed by our Creator with certain unalienable rights, among them life, liberty, and the pursuit of happiness. It's the insistence that these rights, while self-evident, have never been self-executing; that We, the People, through the instrument of our democracy, can form a more perfect union.

What a radical idea. A great gift that our Founders gave to us: The freedom to chase our individual dreams through our sweat and toil and imagination, and the imperative to strive together, as well, to achieve a common good, a greater good.

For 240 years, our nation's call to citizenship has given work and purpose to each new generation. It's what led patriots to choose republic over tyranny, pioneers to trek west, slaves to brave that makeshift railroad to freedom. It's what pulled immigrants and refugees across oceans and the Rio Grande. (Applause.) It's what pushed women to reach for the ballot. It's what powered workers to organize. It's why GIs gave their lives at Omaha Beach and Iwo Jima, Iraq and Afghanistan. And why men and women from Selma to Stonewall were prepared to give theirs, as well. (Applause.) [...]

To begin with, our democracy won't work without a sense that everyone has economic opportunity. And the good news is that today the economy is growing again. Wages, incomes, home values, and retirement accounts are all rising again. Poverty is falling again. (Applause.) The wealthy are paying a fairer share of taxes even as the stock market shatters records. The unemployment rate is near a 10-year low. The uninsured rate has never, ever been lower. (Applause.) Health care costs are rising at the slowest rate in 50 years. And I've said and I mean it – if anyone can put together a plan that is demonstrably better than the improvements we've made to our health care system and that covers as many people at less cost, I will publicly support it. (Applause.)

Because that, after all, is why we serve. Not to score points or take credit, but to make people's lives better. (Applause.)

But for all the real progress that we've made, we know it's not enough. [...]

My fellow Americans, it has been the honor of my life to serve you. (Applause.) I won't stop. In fact, I will be right there with you, as a citizen, for all my remaining days. But for now, whether you are young or whether you're young at heart, I do have one final ask of you as your President – the same thing I asked when you took a chance on me eight years ago. I'm asking you to believe. Not in my ability to bring about change – but in yours.

I am asking you to hold fast to that faith written into our founding documents; that idea whispered by slaves and abolitionists; that spirit sung by immigrants and homesteaders and those who marched for justice; that creed reaffirmed by those who planted flags from foreign battlefields to the surface of the moon; a creed at the core of every American whose story is not yet written: Yes, we can. (Applause.)

Yes, we did. Yes, we can. (Applause.)

Thank you. God bless you. May God continue to bless the United States of America. (Applause.)

Barack Obama, 2017, whitehouse.gov

13 **steel mill** a factory which produces steel • 23 **toil** hard work • 34 **to shatter** to break sth into pieces • 49 **creed** set of belief

1.2 Structure

A speech contains three parts: the **introduction**, the **body** and the **conclusion**.

Introduction: In the introduction you express your gratitude for being invited as a speaker; you establish contact with your audience; you want to grab their attention.

You can do this by:
- adressing the audience directly
- creating a positive atmosphere by using humour
- telling an exciting anecdote
- use an easy-going style

a) *Analyse how President Obama establishes contact with the audience in the beginning of his speech (ll. 1–6) and fill in the grid.*

ways of establishing contact	examples from the text
✎	✎
✎	✎
✎	✎

Body: Depending on the topic and purpose of your speech, you can organise the **body** of your speech in chronological or topical order, according to cause and effect, problem and solution, or advantage and disadvantage.

b) *Have a look at the groups of expressions and put them in the gaps in the chart. Try to keep them in mind when producing your own texts.*

- on the one hand … on the other hand, whereas, although, nevertheless, however
- for that reason, as a result, thus, consequently
- ~~after, before, as soon as, by the time, since, until, afterwards, finally, meanwhile~~
- moreover, furthermore, in addition to that, besides
- if, unless, in case of, in the event of, provided that, on the condition that

chronological order	after, before, as soon as, by the time, since, until, afterwards, finally, meanwhile
topical order	✎
cause and effect	✎
problem and solution	✎
advantage and disadvantage	✎

Conclusion: In the conclusion you emphasise the most important point/appeal of your speech and thank the audience for listening.

1.3 Content

Give a short summary of the excerpts from Obama's speech.

In his speech, President Obama ...

1.4 Stylistic devices

Stylistic devices are not only found in literary texts, but they are essential to any type of good writing. Here are some of the most important stylistic devices.

On the level of sounds

Stylistic device	Function/effect	Example
Alliteration: repetition of a sound (usually a consonant) at the beginning of neighbouring words	to give emphasis and stress connections	the *f*irst, the *f*astest and the *f*ittest
Assonance: identical vowel sounds in two or more words	to put emphasis on sth; to coin a memorable phrase	Sw*ee*t dr*ea*ms

On the level of words

Stylistic device	Function/effect	Example
Anaphora: one or more words are repeated at the beginning of neighbouring sentences	to put emphasis on sth	*It is our* city. *It is our* decision. *It is our* future.
Metaphor: a comparison between two objects or ideas, ***without*** a word of comparison ("like", "as" or "as if")	specification	Holidays are heaven.
Simile: a comparison between two objects or ideas, using "like", "as" or "as if"	specification	Holidays are *like* heaven.
Synonyms: two words with the same meaning	to put emphasis on sth	He was ***heavily drunk*** and ***intoxicated***.
Hyperbole: an overstatement/ exaggeration	used to emphasise a particular feeling	I've told you ***a million times*** not to exaggerate.
Personification: something is presented as an active living being	to emphasise the power of something	The sea devoured the ship.

Now use your skills

Analyse the stylistic devices Barack Obama uses and their effect on the reader. Fill in the gaps.

Quote from the text	Stylistic device	Function/effect
"[...] kept me [...], and kept me [...], and kept me [...]" (l.9)	✎	✎
"[...] life, liberty [...]" (l.19)	✎	✎
"[...] slaves to brave [...]" (l.26)	✎	✎

2 Non-fictional texts: Newspaper article

'Affluenza' teen Ethan Couch sentenced to 720 days in jail

Lawyers given two weeks to convince judge to change his mind about sentence for 19-year-old's killing of four people in 2013 drunk driving accident.

The Texas teen who used the now infamous "affluenza" defense after killing four people in a drunk driving accident will serve nearly two years in jail, a judge ruled on Wednesday. The ruling came after an hour of arguments about whether a judge in an adult court had the ability to sentence Ethan Couch to serve time in jail for violating a probation imposed on him by a juvenile court in 2015.

Couch had previously pleaded guilty to killing four people in the 2013 accident. But after his defense team argued that he suffered from "affluenza" – which they said meant that he was unable to tell right from wrong after being raised by wealthy parents – he was sentenced to rehab and 10 years' probation. The sentence drew much criticism from the victims' families and local law enforcement officials.

Couch is currently accused of violating his probation – which prohibits him from drinking, using drugs and driving – after he fled to Mexico in December with his mother after a video appeared on social media showing Couch at a party with alcohol.

After the video surfaced, Couch's probation officer was unable to get in touch with him and a warrant for his arrest was issued. Couch and his mother were arrested 11 days later in Mexico, after he used his phone to place an order for pizza. Couch has been in jail since his arrest.

Couch, who turned 19 on Monday, made his first appearance in adult court on Wednesday in Fort Worth. It is unclear if the time he has spent in jail awaiting the hearing will count towards his sentence.

Much of Wednesday's hearing was focused on whether the judge should sentence Couch to 180 or 120 days in jail. Prosecutors argued that since there were four different victims in the 2013 accident, this should be treated as four different violations.

The defense disagreed, arguing that the case should be treated the way it was in juvenile court.

Four stacked sentences – each for 180 days in jail – is the most that judge Wayne Salvant could give. After he announced the sentence, Salvant told lawyers that they had two weeks to submit additional information that could be used to change his mind.

After serving out his sentence, Couch will also have to finish the 10-year probation. The terms remain the same: no drinking, no drugs, no driving. He must comply with any blood, urine and breathalyzer tests. Additionally, if Couch seeks to leave the nearby counties, he would first need to obtain a permission. If Couch violated his probation as an adult, he could be sent to prison for up to 40 years – 10 years for each person he killed in 2013.

Salvant also urged the lawyers in the case to not voice their opinions about how the case ought to be handled in the press. The reason, according to Salvant, is that Couch's case is "intertwined" with his mother's.

Tonya Couch faces charge of hindering the apprehension of a felon and faces between two and 10 years in prison if convicted. She is currently under house arrest.

6 **probation** release of a sentenced criminal from prison under terms of good behavior • 11 **rehab** *(informal)* the process of learning to live without drug consumption • 28 **stacked** separated • 39 **apprehension** arrest • 39 **felon** criminal

2.1 Getting started: Basics about newspaper articles

We are confronted with a wide range of different newspapers from all around the world. On the one hand there are **quality** or **posh papers**. They separate information and opinion so that the reader can form his/her own view. On the other hand there are **popular papers**. They often mix information and opinion, offering the reader a ready-made opinion. All kinds of newspapers contain different types of articles, e.g.:

News stories	• provide information on current events which interest the readers. • different features make news newsworthy: ◦ the news deals with matters close to the reader ◦ the news refers to current events ◦ the news presents very new or unusual news items (e.g. medical discoveries, mother at 65) ◦ the news reports about sensational topics (e.g. scandals, tragedies, disasters) ◦ the news informs about conflicts (e.g. political controversies, ethical problems, e.g. abortion) A **news report** is a news story only based on facts. It avoids additional information about the event and the story behind it and also the writer's personal opinion.
Comments	• offer views on current issues and can be divided into subtypes: ◦ **Editorials** contain comments which are based on a newspaper's tendency (liberal or conservative paper) and are therefore close to the views of the reader who buys this paper. ◦ The so-called **op-eds** (opposite editorial or opinion editorial) give second or different opinions (opposed to the newspaper's tendency) on a subject. ◦ Journalists who work as **columnists** regularly write their **columns** (short essays on different topics the journalist is free to choose).
Human interest stories	• illustrate general problems with the help of one individual case, thus arousing sympathy (e.g. victims of an earthquake, victims of diseases).

Now use your skills

According to the information given in the table above, what kind of newspaper article is the article you read at the beginning of the chapter?

____

____

2.2 Structure

The first paragraph – the lead, often in bold print – answers the **wh-questions**: Who?, What?, When?, Where? and Why? The information within the article is arranged according to the **inverted pyramid**: the most important information comes first, less important information towards the end of the article. So if the editor shortens the article or the reader stops reading, the most important facts are still provided.

Tip !

Inverted pyramid

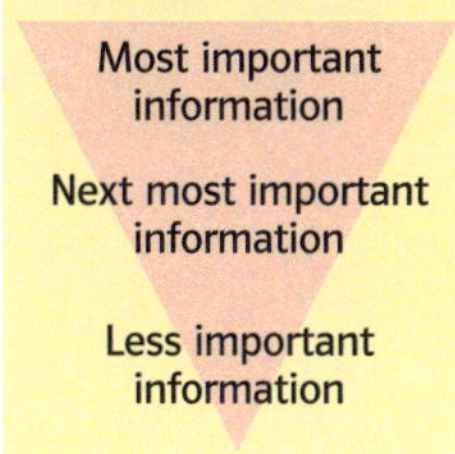

a) *Briefly sum up the article by Jana Kasperkevic.*

The article written by Jana Kasperkevic and published …

____

____

____

____

Tip !

Structure of a newspaper article:
- Title or headline
- Lead or opening sentence
- Body (starts with the most important information/ wh-questions)

Tip !

It can be a help to write key terms in the margin of the text and use these notes for your analysis. Use general terms – do not write a second summary.

b) *Analyse the structure of the article. Fill in the chart.*

	Use general terms	Exemplify
ll.1–7	wh-questions are answered	Teenager (Ethan Couch); Texas; killed four people in a drunk driving accident; sentenced to almost two years in prison
ll.8–12	background information on case history	✎
ll.13–19	✎	✎
ll.20–27	✎	✎
ll.28–35	✎	✎
ll.36–40	✎	✎

2.3 Language and line of argument

Now use your skills

Analyse the author's way of presenting Ethan Couch's case.

Step 1: First examine the language focusing on the register and the vocabulary. Note down your results.

> **Tip !**
> News stories in quality papers like *The Guardian* provide objective and unbiased information. Thus the reader can form his own opinion. The way of presenting the news and the selection of details may reveal the journalist's attitude, however.

Step 2: Then analyse the line of arguments. Note down arguments supporting a harsh or a lenient sentence for Couch.

Arguments in favour of a lenient sentence	Arguments in favour of a harsh sentence
Defense: Couch suffers from 'affluenza'	✎
	✎
	✎

Step 3: The text offers the reader detailed information about the case. What effect do the details have on the reader? Fill in the list below.

Details	Effect
a video on the internet shows Couch drinking alcohol at a party in Mexico	presents Couch as unreasonable, making the same mistakes again supports the demand for a harsh sentence
the judge can sentence Couch to a maxium of 180 days in jail for each victim	✎
the judge urged the lawyers not to express their opinion about the case to the press since another trial concerning the mother still has to be dealt with	✎

Step 4: Conclusion of Step 1–3: How does the author present Couch's case?

3 Non-fictional texts: Review

3.1 Getting started: The nature of reviews

Everybody's time and money are limited, so if you want to go to the cinema, for example, you usually get some information first. Reviews are the typical source of information on which film to watch.

Apart from films, can you think of other things that are reviewed?

3.2 Structure

The form of reviews can vary as widely as the sources where you find them: They range from very informal and short reviews in the Internet to well-written and complicated ones written by professional critics, for example in quality newspapers or specialised magazines. All reviews, however, follow the basic structure of **introduction – body – conclusion.**

a) *Match the terms with the definitions:*

introduction | body | conclusion

The …	consists of a short plot outline (where appropriate) and the writer's opinion about central aspects (depending on the type of item reviewed, see below), supported by facts and examples.
The …	often starts with a joke or anecdote to catch the reader's interest. Alternatively it describes the writer's first reaction or states clearly what is being reviewed (in the case of concerts, shows or plays this includes the exact location and date of the performance).
The …	sums up the writer's view and usually includes a recommendation or a warning (often also a rating, such as four stars out of five).

Now use your skills

b) *Look at the following lines from a film review on* The Lord of the Rings. *Are they taken from the introduction, the body or the conclusion? Find the typical features and explain their function.*

Seven years in the making, three Christmases in the screening, nine-and-a-half hours in the telling, Peter Jackson's *Lord of the Rings* trilogy finished with the closing of a round yellow door, a soft fade-out and the words "The End" written in gold Celtic font. Almost inevitably, the moment was marked with a storm of applause around the cinema. But was the audience gathered at the film's London press show applauding out of admiration or relief? Chances are that it was a little of both.

By Xan Brooks, © 2003, Guardian News & Media Ltd.

3 **font** *here:* letters

3.3 Content

While the basic structure is the same for all kinds of reviews, the content (especially in the **body**) of a review can be very different depending on what is being reviewed. In the list below you will find the most important contents of film, book and theatre reviews:

a) *There are some gaps in the chart. Think of more details and fill in the gaps.*

The body of a film review:	• **genre:** Is it a comedy, a romance, a thriller etc.? Does it fit the genre, or maybe even expand or change it? etc. • **director:** What has he/she directed before? Is he/she experienced in this kind of film? • • • **technical elements (such as editing, lighting, special effects, sound, use of camera):** Are they well executed? Are they used to increase the intended effect of the film or just for their own sake?
The body of a book review:	• • **genre, plot:** a crime novel, a fantasy epic, a collection of short stories, etc.? • **language, style, point of view** •
The body of a review on a theatre production:	• **detailed information about the location** • • **director, actors** •

Tip !

Since reviews are such a free type of text and usually space is very limited, hardly any reviews contain all of the typical information. The order in which these elements are presented can also vary greatly.

Now use your skills

b) *Look at an excerpt from the body and the conclusion of the film review on the following page. Which topics are discussed?*

[…] The last part of Jackson's trilogy is both the best and the worst of *The Lord of the Rings*. It begins in gripping fashion, with a crash-course biography of Gollum (Andy Serkis), perhaps the most purely engrossing of all Tolkien's characters. From here we hop into the main action of a movie which is effectively a three-and-a-bit-hour climax, as the armies of men ride into battle against the orcs and Frodo (Elijah Wood) presses towards Mount Doom with the "One Ring To Rule Them All" hanging heavy round his neck.

The Return of the King is ablaze with brilliant set-pieces. True to the form of its predecessors, it's a picture painted across a mammoth canvas, whether pivoting around the white city of Minas Tirith or rustling up what could well be the most mesmerising, perfectly staged battle scenes that I've ever seen at the cinema (or anywhere else for that matter). Even so, the film boasts its share of intense, intimate moments too, with a pungent father-son drama between Denethor (John Noble) and his martyred son Faramir (David Wenham), and the ongoing fascination of the love-triangle that is Gollum, Frodo and Sam (Sean Astin). […]

Despite its flaws, *The Return of the King* is a rich and rousing finale to one of the great sagas of our age. Because in the end I do think there is a greatness to this trilogy. It has captivated us in a way that most other movies can only dream of, conjured up a world and made it real. But now it is over, finished, kaput. Now, at long last, we can move on.

By Xan Brooks, © 2003, Guardian News & Media Ltd.

2 **gripping** thrilling • 3 **engrossing** absorbing, captivating • 7 **ablaze** shining, brilliant • 8 **canvas** cloth, material • 8 **pivoting** moving • 9 **mesmerising** captivating, fascinating • 11 **pungent** bitter • 14 **flaw** weakness • 17 **kaput** *here:* over

3.4 Stylistic devices

As mentioned before reviews are a relatively free type of text and the writers often don't stick to fixed rules. The form of a review depends on its purpose and target group. A comment on a film on an Internet website does not require a special form. Everybody can present his or her opinion there.

The review taken from *The Guardian* you read in this chapter certainly belongs to the group of the more elaborate reviews. Due to this reason, its style is different from the reviews you might have read on the Internet on your own.

Fill in the gaps with more stylistic devices from the text and explain their function.

"the ***best*** and the ***worst***" (l.1)	paradox → ✎
"***h***anging ***h***eavy" (l.6)	✎
"***p***icture ***p***ainted" (l.8)	✎
"***i***ntense, ***i***ntimate" (l.11)	✎
✎	✎
✎	✎

In the next chapter you will look at fictional texts. Some of the things you have learned in this chapter apply to fictional texts as well.

Text analysis: C Fictional texts

On the one hand, analysing fictional texts is very similar to analysing non-fictional ones: You look at the structure, the language and the function of a text. Many things you have used on the previous pages, for example stylistic devices, will be useful here, too. But on the other hand, there are some aspects which are only found in fictional texts: in prose, drama and poetry. In this chapter, you will learn about each of these and have the opportunity to practise directly with texts.

1 Prose

1.1 Getting started: Describing the action

For analysing novels and short stories you need to know some basic terms to describe the action of the story or book.

a) *Make sure that you are familiar with these basic terms, then read the short story "Mr. Mumsford" below.*

Setting	the time and place of the action (due to its shortness, a short story usually has only one setting); it often helps to create a certain atmosphere	
Theme	the main topic, the central subject which gives meaning to the story/novel as a whole	
Plot	the structure of the action; the main events in the story/novel – it says what happens in which order, and why; a novel usually has a complex plot which develops in different settings with a large number of characters	
Structure	**beginning**	A prose text may start with an immediate beginning (directly with a situation) or slowly with an exposition (= introduction) which gives the information necessary to understand the events which follow.
	main part	A short story typically – presents a conflict or a crisis. – leads up to a climax or a turning-point. – focuses on a character's thoughts and emotions in a situation. Novels are much longer and more complex, so their main part can include several different conflicts, turning points and characterisations.
	ending	A prose text may have an open, a happy/unhappy or a surprise ending.

Larry French: "Mr. Mumsford"

Bibs, the janitor, had never killed a man before. He'd raised rabbits as a boy and killed one now and then for supper. A quick blow to the back of the neck, and it was done. He was not a particularly intelligent man and was not suffering from guilt or any philosophical questions about what he was going to do. He had come to the small southern school as a janitor twenty-seven years ago. On his first day at school, he had worn a pair of old bib overalls and thus earned the nickname of Bibs. This was the reason he had come to kill the principal who was working late in his office down the hall. Earlier in the evening, Bibs had gone into the equipment room and picked out the largest baseball bat he could find. He then went and hid in a space between the green metal lockers that lined the hallways. At a little past ten the principal walked out of his office, locked it, and started down the hall. Bibs stepped out in front of him.

"Say, Bibs," asked the principal. "What are you doing here this time of night?"

Beads of sweat stood out on Bibs' forehead, and he clenched the bat with both hands. He was six feet tall, very black, and towered over the principal.

"I come to kill you," said Bibs.

"But why? What have I ever done to you?"

"Just what you called me is why!" said Bibs. "Nobody in this school, including you, has ever bothered to learn my real name. Onliest person knows my real name is that woman signs my check, and even she puts it in an envelope marked BIBS. The kids should learn my name in four years. Hell, I know more'n half of their names and where they live. This morning I stopped a couple of 'em and asked 'em did they know my real name, and they looked at me like I was crazy. That's why I come to kill you!"

The principal was a short man anyway, but now his shoulders slumped even further, and he looked sad and confused.

Tip !
To help you with the tasks later on you can underline and make notes whenever you find out something about the action.

"Well," he said. "Well, what is your name?" "Ralph Mumsford," said Bibs. "Mumsford's a strange name for a black man to have." said the principal. "It's English, isn't it?" "I don't know." "You should look it up," said the principal. "You should go over to the school library and look it up. Say, lookee here, if I promise me and all my teachers call you by your real name from now on, will you not kill me?"

Bibs thought for a moment, seemed to waver, and then said, "Well, that seems fair. You do that, and I won't have to kill you."

The principal looked tired.

"You been working too many hours," said Bibs. "A Christian man ought to always eat the supper meal with his wife."

The principal sighed and said, "I do believe you're right, Mr. Mumsford. I do believe you have a point there." Then he turned and walked down the dark corridor toward the green exit sign leading out to the playground.

1 **janitor** the person whose job it is to look after a building • 1 **to raise** *here:* to keep and feed • 2 **blow** hard hit • 5 **bib overalls** Arbeitslatzhose • 5 **thus** *(formal)* therefore • 6 **nickname** informal name used instead of sb's real name • **principal** (AE) headmaster (BE) • 8 **baseball bat** wooden stick used for hitting a baseball • 9 **to line sth** *here:* to form a row along sth • 13 **bead** small drop • 13 **forehead** part of the face above the eyes and below the hair • 14 **to tower over sb** to be a lot taller than sb • 18 **not to bother** not to think it necessary to do sth • 19 **check** (AE) *here:* paycheck • 23 **to slump** to move downwards, to drop • 31 **lookee** *(informal)* imperative of *to look* • 33 **to waver** to hesitate • 39 **to have a point** to be right

Now use your skills

Refer to the terms above and the **Useful phrases** below when dealing with these questions:

b) *What is "Mr. Mumsford" about (setting, theme, etc.)? What lesson does the story teach?*

c) *Outline the incident the story describes.* (→ see also p.13, Summary writing)

Useful phrases: Action !

The story	• is set in a certain environment at a certain time. • deals with the theme of … • describes the memorable meeting of two people/a shocking event/a surprise discovery. • presents a moral problem/a conflict between … and … • is divided into … parts.
The theme	• is the conflict between … and … • may be a human emotion such as love or sorrow, or its absence.
The setting	• may be the immediate surroundings (location/scenery) or in a wider sense the region/the society in which the action is placed. • creates/evokes a certain atmosphere, e.g. of calm and security. • may have a symbolic meaning.
The atmosphere	• may be calm/cosy/friendly/relaxed/warm/informal. • may be hostile/oppressive/tense or intimate/romantic.
The plot	• focuses on the development of a relationship. • is based on the escalating conflict between … and …
The conflict/ crisis/critical situation	• arises from sth/occurs when … • may be serious/violent/open/public/internal/hidden. • is caused or provoked by sth. • can be avoided or prevented by doing sth. • should be handled calmly and solved peacefully.

1.2 Characters: Characterisation

a) *Read the descriptions, and then match them with the correct type of character.*

antagonist | ~~protagonist/hero/heroine~~ | minor character | flat character | round character

Tip !
In a literary text, you say 'characters', not '~~person/people~~'.

Type of character	Definition
protagonist/hero/heroine	the main/central character
✎	a character who can be described in a few words; his/her behaviour is predictable, as he/she does not develop or learn, and never surprises the reader
✎	a less important character
✎	the enemy of the protagonist; a character who is opposed to, or in conflict with, the main character
✎	a life-like, complex individual; he/she may be shown in different moods and usually develops/undergoes a learning process in the course of the action

Characters in a prose text can be presented in two ways: The narrator or a character in the text directly tells the reader what the person is like (**direct characterisation**). Or the reader has to find out what a character is like by what this character does, says, thinks or feels (**indirect characterisation**).

b) *What does the information below tell you about the character?*
Fill in the grid, but be careful: There may be several different interpretations!

Information on what a character ...	Possible (indirect) characterisations ("reading between the lines")
... is called: His friends called him "buffalo".	He is strong, pig-headed, ...
... wears: Even at the age of 50, he still wore his jeans and a T-shirt on all occasions.	✎
... does: She touched his hair.	She has tender feelings for him; she loves him; she admires his hairstyle; ...
... did: When he came home from war, he spent five days driving his father's car back and forth through town.	✎
... says: "Have I ever said that I like you?"	✎
... thinks: The men in the room were queuing to dance with her, but still she believed herself ugly and uninteresting.	✎
... feels: It was heaven. I felt like I was God.	✎

Now use your skills

c) *Read the story "Mr. Mumsford" again. Fill in the first column of the grid on the next page with the basic information about the protagonist Mr. Mumsford. Focus only on what you learn through direct characterisation: What is explicitly said in the story?*

d) *Then, in the second column, add the corresponding information about the second character. Do you find this information in the text (direct characterisation) or is it indirectly given?*

e) *There may be different reasons for an author not to give the name of a character, e.g.:*
- *He/she is just a minor or background character.*
- *His/her name is not known to the other characters.*
- *He/she is a flat character who is identified by one main character trait.*
- *He/she is not an individual in the story but represents a larger group of people.*

In your opinion, which reason (or combination of reasons) is a plausible one for not giving the name of the principal?

Basic information	Mr. Mumsford: direct characterisation	The principal: direct or indirect characterisation?
name	Ralph Mumsford (nickname: Bibs)	
skin colour	✎	indirect: he is not aware of the unfair treatment of his employee; probably white
job	✎	✎
height	✎	✎
intelligence	✎	✎

f) *Who is the protagonist in this story? Can the other character be called his antagonist?*

____

____

____

____

g) *Are Mr. Mumsford and the principal flat or round characters (or something in between these extremes)? Why?*

____

____

____

1.3 Characters: Relationships

a) *These phrases will help you when you want to talk or write about relationships. Fill in the blanks below, and then highlight the phrases you were unfamiliar with. If in doubt, use a dictionary.*

Match these five verbs with a verb similar in meaning when used with 'relationship':
~~develop~~ • manage • end • maintain • improve

to build up/ develop ______
to continue/ ______
to handle/ ______
to strengthen/ ______
to break off/ ______
→ a relationship

Match these five adjectives with the two adjectives with a similar meaning when describing a 'relationship':
professional • close • superficial • long-term • strained

a
friendly/trusting/ ______
steady/lasting/ ______
working/business/ ______
brief/casual/ ______
poor/troubled/ ______
→ relationship

Use a dictionary to find the missing prepositions and fill them in.

mutual respect for ______ /acceptance ______ the other
understanding/empathy ______ each other
closeness/harmony ______ x and y
little/shallow communication ______ x and y
to keep close contact ______ sb
to share information ______ sb
to show real interest ______ sb

relationship based ______ equality
lack ______ respect and acceptance
emotional distance ______ x and y
little interest ______ the other
to keep one's distance ______ sb
to withdraw ______ sb
to put pressure ______ sb

Now use your skills

b) *Practise the phrases from page 32 by describing some typical relationships in the boxes below.*

c) *Then use some of these phrases to describe the relationship between the two characters in "Mr. Mumsford".*

Relationship between …	Description of a positive relationship	Description of a negative relationship
parents and children	close, loving, intense communication, …	✎
teacher and pupil	✎	✎
employer and employee	✎	✎
Mr. Mumsford and the principal	✎	

1.4 Characters: Attitudes and feelings

a) *Make sure you know these phrases. Highlight those you do not know. If in doubt, use a dictionary.*

Useful phrases: Attitudes !

to have an attitude to(wards) sb – to notice a change of/in attitude			
to accept sb	to reject sb	sensitive	understanding
to trust sb	to ignore sb	polite	respectful
to respect sb	to criticise sb	reserved	indifferent
to admire sb	to mistrust sb	calm	self-controlled

Useful phrases: Feelings !

to express one's	friendly/tender	feelings/emotions
to hide one's	deep/strong	
to evoke	mixed/hurt	
to create/be in a(n)	cheerful/optimistic	mood/state of mind
	angry/desperate	
	thoughtful	

Now use your skills

b) *First impressions: Only on the basis of what you remember about the story "Mr. Mumsford", quickly fill in this grid with expressions from above which you think describe the attitudes/feelings of the two characters in this story.*

	Mr. Mumsford	The principal
attitudes and feelings	✎	✎

c) *Close reading: Now check your memory with a detailed analysis of the characters' attitudes and feelings in the course of the story. On the next page you will find a grid with relevant quotations from the text in the left column. Think about what they reveal about the characters (indirect characterisation) and add your interpretations in the right column. The box with* ***Useful phrases*** *may help you.*

Useful phrases: Dealing with conflicts !

to continue talking	to be at a loss for words
to suggest compromises	to win time
to listen carefully	to hide one's fear
to respond (to sb) calmly	to react (to sb) defensively
to signal understanding for sth	to suppress one's feelings
to ask for motives/reasons	to have feelings of guilt
to make concessions	to defend oneself

Phrases from the text (M = Mr. Mumsford, P = principal)	**Possible comments**
At a little past ten the principal walked out of his office … (ll.9–10)	P takes his work seriously, is conscientious
M: Beads of sweat … clenched the bat … (l.13)	M is nervous, under pressure, tense
M: "I come to kill you …" (l.15)	✎
P: "But why?" (l.16)	✎
M: "Hell, I know more'n half of their names and where they live." (l.20)	✎
P: … his shoulders slumped even further … (l.23)	✎
P: "Well," he said. "Well, …" (l.25)	✎
P: "Mumsford's a strange name for a black man …" (l.27)	✎
P: "You should look it up …" (l.30)	✎
P: "Say, lookee here, …" (l.31)	✎
P: "… if I promise me and all my teachers …" (l.31)	✎
Bibs thought for a moment, seemed to waver, and then said, "Well, that seems fair." (l.33)	✎
M: "A Christian man ought …" (l.36)	✎
P: " I do believe you're right, Mr. Mumsford. I do believe …" (l.38)	✎

1.5 Point of view: Overview

The point of view is extremely important for analysing a prose text, but identifying the correct one can be tricky. The questions in the grid below provide a simple step-by-step approach to the problem.

1. Is there a character in the story speaking as "I"?				
NO → **third-person** point of view			YES → **first-person** point of view	
2. Are you informed (from outside the story) about the emotions and thoughts of . . . ?			**3. Is the narrator (who is a character in the story) . . . ?**	
all characters ↓	one (or two) characters ↓	no character ↓	the protagonist ↓	not the protagonist ↓
omniscient narrator	**selective narrator**	**objective narrator**	**protagonist-narrator**	**witness-narrator**
unlimited perspective	limited perspective		limited perspective	
the omniscient narrator can be neutral, but often comments on and evaluates what happens ("intrusive omniscient narrator")	the selective narrator can also be called "limited omniscient narrator"	the objective narrator is impersonal, i.e. he/she reports from the outside as a "hidden observer"	the protagonist-narrator is the central character of the story	the witness-narrator often is very close to the protagonist (e.g. a friend or relative)

Now use your skills

a) *Identify the point of view in the short story "Mr. Mumsford" with the help of the questions 1 to 3 in the table above. Then fill in the blanks in the short text below.*

________ -person point of view. In the first few lines the ______________ describes Mr. Mumsford's feelings ("was not suffering from guilt" (l.3)) and also knows what is going to happen ("about what he was going to do" (l.4)). He is only reporting the thoughts of one person, so he can be said to be a ____________________. In the rest of the text, however, the narrator is more like a ____________________ and only tells what can be seen or heard (____________________). In both cases, the point of view is _________________.

b) *Here are five variations on the beginning of the short story "The Dragon" by Cynthia Forder (the first one is the original), one for each point of view. Finish the texts or fill in the empty boxes on the right. Note: The second character's name is Kate.*

Text variations of the beginning	Points of view
It was a porch-sitting night, so Bob and I moved out to the swing. Bob liked the swing, and sometimes he rocked it so hard that I felt seasick. We could see the city from the porch. At night, the lights made it look beautiful. The oil refineries looked like castles from a children's book. Some even breathed fire, as if dragons were inside. Bob wasn't looking at the view. Things like that didn't interest him. He was talking about his relatives. He could be so boring. I didn't really hate him. He couldn't help it if he was boring and stupid. […]	

I had been aware of Bob's problems to get along with girls for a very long time. A mother notices these things. So I had second thoughts when visiting my friend Joan whose daughter Kate was just the right age for Bob. *While Joan was preparing tea, I observed the two teens …* ✎	first-person witness-narrator (Bob's mother observes the two teenagers from inside the house)
It was a porch-sitting night, so Bob and Kate moved out to the swing. Bob was a 16-year-old computer nerd with little experience with girls and he was happy being invited over for a visit by Kate's mother, who was hopeful that Bob might help Kate with a mathematics project. Bob, however, had very different intentions but found it hard to find a common topic to start with. The swing – so he thought – was a good place to begin a romance, and Kate seemed to like the view of the city at night. Sadly, Bob could not have been more wrong about Kate's present state of mind. At a loss for words, Bob was rocking the swing so hard that Kate felt seasick. If she had known of Bob's surprise visit, she would certainly have found a good excuse to avoid this meeting with a boy she found utterly unattractive and boring. […]	✎
It was a porch-sitting night, so Bob and Kate moved out to the swing. Bob rocked the swing very hard. In the distance, … ✎	third-person objective narrator (like a camera which is only recording what can be seen and heard)
It was a porch-sitting night, so Bob and Kate moved out to the swing. Bob liked the swing, and sometimes he rocked it so hard that Kate felt seasick. They could see the city from the porch. At night, the lights made it look beautiful. Kate thought that the oil refineries looked like castles from a children's book. Some even breathed fire, as if dragons were inside. Kate, however, didn't feel romantic at all. Bob wasn't looking at the view. Things like that didn't seem to interest him. He was talking about his relatives. Kate was bored. She didn't really hate Bob, she simply didn't feel attracted to him. He couldn't help it if he was boring and stupid. […]	✎

1.6 Point of view: Reliability and identification

The point of view chosen by the author has consequences for …
- the degree of objectivity and reliability of the information: Which narrators are fairly objective/reliable, which are necessarily rather subjective/unreliable?
- the degree of identification with the characters: How does a narrator influence who the reader identifies with? How strongly can he/she identify with the characters?

a) *Think about the different points of view and what they mean for the reliability of the narrator and the identification with the characters. Then fill in the table below.*

Narrator	Objectivity/reliability of information	Identification
first-person (protagonist or witness)	very subjective, usually unreliable	✎
third-person omniscient	✎	✎
third-person selective	✎	✎
third-person objective	✎	✎

Now use your skills

Answer the following questions. The **Useful phrases** below can help you.

b) *The author may change the point of view in a novel. How could he/she do this, and why?*

c) *Which type of narrator do you personally prefer when reading a short story or a novel? Why?*

Useful phrases: Narrators !

The author	• is not identical with the narrator. • uses/employs a … narrator. • makes use of a third-person point of view.
The narrator	• is the voice or character who tells the story. • tells the story in the first or third person. • can have a limited or an unlimited perspective.
A first-person narrator	• is him- or herself a character in the story, speaks as "I". • takes part in the action as a witness/an observer or is the central character. • is limited to what he himself knows/experiences/learns from sb else.
A third-person narrator	• is not a character in the story. • refers to the characters in the story as "he", "she" or "they" or by their names. • decides to what extent he informs the reader about the action and the characters.
The omniscient narrator	• enters the minds of the characters at will. • can add his own comments and explanations.
The selective narrator	• makes the reader see everything through the eyes of one character. • confines himself to what is experienced, thought and felt by a single character.
The objective narrator	• is impersonal, unobtrusive, self-effacing. • presents only the external action and not the characters' thoughts and feelings. • does not add comments and judgements.

1.7 Point of view: Function

a) *Fill in the correct point of view.* (→ see p.35 for help)

Narrator	Functions/consequences
third-person omniscient narrator	The advantage of this point of view lies in the reader's access to the characters' feelings and thoughts. The reader gets comprehensive characterisations and interpretations. If the narrator is overly intrusive with his/her comments and evaluation, the reader might be made a passive "consumer" of the narration without any room left for interpretation.
first-p - pro	The reader follows the course of events through the eyes of the central character who tells his/her story in the first person. In this way the reader experiences the story with a great deal of immediacy and is constantly informed about the protagonist's thoughts and feelings. Not surprisingly, the reader is emotionally strongly involved and very likely to identify with the narrator (identification figure). The perspective is clearly limited; the description may be one-sided and to some extent subjective.
objectiv	This point of view demands the reader's full attention and constant "reading between the lines". Without any access to the characters' minds, the reader has to draw his/her own conclusions about their motives and thoughts. The limitation of this point of view is that only neutral description and dialogue are possible.
selektiv	With this point of view, the omniscient narrator has decided to only inform the reader about what is going on in the mind of one or two characters. This means limited, and possibly biased/unreliable, information about the events and other characters. On the other hand, it may create suspense through gap-filling and encourage interpretation.
first-p →	The narrator is part of the action, though not always at its centre. He gives (possibly sketchy or even unreliable) information and makes comments as an observer from outside. As this narrator has only limited first-hand information, he often has to rely on hearsay, gossip or rumours. The reader needs to trust the narrator, but knows that he does not get a complete picture of the events.

Now use your skills

b) *Now try to find your own words for the advantages and disadvantages of each point of view and write them into the empty boxes below.* (→ The five different story beginnings on pp.35–36 may help.)

What are the functions/consequences of each point of view? What are the advantages/disadvantages for the reader?				
omniscient narrator	selective narrator	objective narrator	protagonist-narrator	witness-narrator

c) *With this information in the background, try to describe the influence which the point of view has on the reader's perception of the two characters in the short story "Mr. Mumsford".* (→ The answer to a) on p.35 is a good starting point.)

2 Poetry

2.1 Getting started: Basic terms concerning form

In this chapter you are going to look at poetry. It has a reputation for 'being difficult' as regards the form as well as the ideas expressed. The following pages will help make it seem less complex.

a) *What do you expect? What makes a poem a poem? Think for yourself for a second and note down your thoughts.*

___

___

___

___

___

___

b) *Read the following terms and definitions. Which term fits which definition? Fill in the gaps.*

metre | foot | emotive language | rhythm | ~~stanza/verse~~ | imagery | rhyme

In a traditional poem you might expect …	term
a group of lines of poetry forming a unit	stanza/verse
language that produces pictures in the minds of people reading or listening	✎
use of words in a poem or song that have the same sound, especially at the end of lines	✎
the arrangement of strong and weak stresses in lines of poetry that produces the rhythm	✎
the use of words and expressions which have particular connotations in order to appeal to the reader's emotions and influence him or her to react in a particular way	✎
the arrangement of stressed or unstressed syllables in writing to produce a certain flow of sound	✎
a group of stressed and unstressed syllables within a line of poetry, e.g. iamb	✎

Tip !
'imagery' has no plural:
In general, the imagery of the poem is …
But: The two images in line 5 express …

Knowing the basic terms, you will now deal with two different poems – a modern one by Frank A. Cross, Jr. and a rather traditional one by William Shakespeare.

Modern poetry: Frank A. Cross, Jr. "Rice will grow again"

We were walking
On the dikes
Like damn fools -
Steppin over dud rounds.
* * *
Mitch was steppin light
When he saw the farmer.
The farmer:
With black shirt
And shorts.
Up to his knees
In the muck
Rice shoots in one hand,
The other darting
Under the water
And into the muck
To plant new life.

Mitch saw the farmer's hand
Going down again
With another
Shoot
But the hand
Never came up
Again –
After Mitch
Ripped the farmer up the middle
With a burst of sixteen.
We passed the farmer,
As we walked along the dike, and
I saw rice shoots
Still clutched in one hand.
He bubbled strange words
Through the blood
In his mouth.
Bong, the scout,
Told us the farmer
Said:
"Damn you
The rice will
Grow again!"
* * *
Sometimes,
On dark nights
In Kansas,
The farmer comes to
Mitch's bed:
And plants rice shoots
all around.

2 **dike** (also dyke) long thick wall built to keep water back and prevent flooding • 4 **dud round** *Blindgängereinschlag* • 5 **to step light** to go step by step and very carefully, e.g. because of danger or not to be heard • 11 **muck** *(informal)* dirt or mud • 12 **shoot** 1. *here*: very young plant seedling of rice 2. the act of shooting • 13 **to dart** to move suddenly and quickly • 25 **to rip up** to tear sth violently • 26 **burst of sixteen** the number of shots fired at the same time from an M-16, the standard automatic rifle used by the American forces in Vietnam after 1966 • 30 **to clutch** to hold sth tightly • 34 **scout** *here*: a Vietnamese soldier sent ahead to get information about the enemy's position/strength etc. • 42 **Kansas** agricultural state in the US on the Great Plains

Now use your skills

c) *Read the poem "Rice will grow again" carefully. Which of the elements of poetry mentioned above do you find in the text? The following phrases will help you to express your findings in a short text.*

Tip !

At first sight a lot of modern, 20th-century poems look like prose texts because they often have no regular rhyme scheme and no regular metre. This phenomenon is called free verse.

Useful phrases: Form !

The poem	• consists of/is divided into/is made up of/comprises … stanzas/sections/lines … • has an introductory/middle/concluding stanza/section. • has an unusual layout. • follows a clear rhyme scheme. • has a/is based on a regular metre/a monotonous rhythm/ a regular rhythmical pattern. • is an example of unrhymed verse/free verse.
Rhyme	• The arrangement of the rhymes is … (e.g. aabb). • The rhyme scheme is regular/irregular. • A number of lines do not rhyme at all. • Lines x and y rhyme.
The poet	• employs/makes use of complex imagery/highly emotive language/etc. • aims to convey/to get across/to express poetically a certain message.

2.2 A modern poem: Content

You have found out that "Rice will grow again" is a modern poem in free verse, lacking most of the characteristics one would expect to find in poetry. Now let us concentrate on its content. Wh-questions help you to find out the most important information:

Read the poem two or three times and look up all the unknown words so that you can understand the text. Then answer the following questions. Find quotes to support your answers.

Tip !
The speaker in a poem is not identical with the poet:
The speaker = the voice speaking as 'I' in a poem.
The poet = Frank A. Cross, Jr.

Questions	Quotes from the text	Interpretation
Who is speaking?	*Find more quotes:* "We were walking" (l.1) "Mitch was steppin light" (l.5) ✎	*Fill in the gaps:* The speaker is a member of a group consisting of ________________ people: the speaker, ________________ and Bong, the scout. Bong seems to be ________________ because he speaks the same language as the ________________ . The speaker and his friend seem to be ________________ soldiers on patrol.
Who is being addressed?	no direct address	✎
What kind of situation is presented?	*Find more quotes:* past tense: "We were walking on the dikes" (ll.1–2) "When he saw the farmer" (l.6) ✎ present tense: "On dark nights In Kansas, The farmer comes […]" (ll.41–43)	The first 40 lines deal with an event that took place in the past in Vietnam. The speaker, a fellow soldier and a Vietnamese scout were on patrol … ✎
What is the theme of the poem?		✎

2.3 A modern poem: Language

After you have looked at the content of a poem in detail, examine the language carefully. The language includes choice of words, as well as the sentence structure.

a) *Before you take another look at "Rice will grow again" make sure you are familiar with the following phrases to help you turn your notes into text.*

Useful phrases: The language !

- It consists of/is divided into/is made up of/comprises … stanzas/sections/lines …
- The vocabulary is colloquial/simple/concrete/difficult/elevated/abstract.
- The words (mainly) belong to the word field of …/the areas of …/the themes of …
- The poet uses/employs/makes use of
- The repetition of the words '…' stresses/emphasises/underlines …/conveys a feeling of …/ contributes to …/creates a … atmosphere.
- The word '…' is contrasted with '…'/contrasts with '…'.
- There is a strong contrast/an antithesis between '…' and '…'.
- The word '…' suggests/implies …
- The long/short sentences slow down/quicken the pace of the poem.
- End-stopped lines slow down/run-on lines quicken the pace of the poem.
- Exclamations/(rhetorical) questions are used to convey the speaker's feelings/emotions/mood of …

Now use your skills

The following questions can be used to guide you through the analysis of any poem.

b) *Take a look at "Rice will grow again" and fill in the gaps with the corresponding information. Answer the questions by quoting from the text. Try to explain the function/the effect of what you have found out.*

1. *What is striking striking about the choice of words (e.g. are there different speech levels/do certain word classes dominate)?*

Language of the poem	Function/effect
simple, concrete sometimes informal, e.g. "damn" (l.3, l.37) or "muck" (l.11, l.15)	makes the situation that is presented appear more realistic, the speaker (soldier) becomes more authentic

2. *What field or theme do the words mainly belong to (e.g. nature, religion)?*

Language of the poem	Function/effect

3. *What repetitions can you find?*

Language of the poem	Function/effect

4. *What kind of contrasts are created in the poem?*

Language of the poem	Function/effect

5. *Are any of the words ambiguous (i.e. do they have more than one meaning)?*

Language of the poem	Function/effect
✎	✎

6. *What is the sentence structure like?*

Language of the poem	Function/effect
✎	✎

7. *What kinds of sentences (statements, questions and exclamations) are mainly used?*

Language of the poem	Function/effect
✎	✎

c) *When you have completed task b), look at everything you have found out about the poem so far. Then characterise its tone (i.e. the speaker's attitude towards his theme). What does the language express about the characters? These expressions may help you:*

Useful phrases: The tone !

The tone is:

- serious/matter-of-fact/sober/calm
- melancholy/sad/depressed/disappointed/gloomy/resigned
- cheerful/joking/playful/ironical
- bitter/angry/cynical/accusing
- reveals/reflects the speaker's feelings

The tone is calm and matter-of-fact. The speaker ...

2.4 Glossary of literary terms: Sound and rhythm

This list contains the most important literary terms. They can be a help when dealing with all kinds of poetry. Most poetry is meant to be heard as well as read. Therefore, sound devices and rhythm play an important part (especially in traditional poetry).

Name	Definition	Example	Function
Rhyme	the likeness of sounds in two or more words; words rhyme when their accented vowels and all following sounds are identical		to achieve a pleasant sound and to underline a rhythmical pattern; to make verse memorable
End rhyme	a rhyme occurring at the end of a line	"The music in my heart I ***bore*** Long after it was heard no ***more***" (W. Wordsworth)	
Internal rhyme	a rhyme occurring within a verse-line	"O fl**ee**t sw**ee**t swallow" (W. B. Yeats)	
Rhyme scheme	the arrangement of end rhymes in a poem, indicated by small letters of the alphabet, e.g. aabb	alternate rhyme: abab enclosed rhyme: abba couplets: aabb	to stress the connection between ideas/statements
Alliteration	repetition of a sound (usually a consonant) at the beginning of neighbouring words	"***L***et us go forth and ***l***ead the ***l***and we ***l***ove." (John F. Kennedy)	to give emphasis and stress connections
Assonance	identical vowel sounds in two or more words	Sw**ee**t dr***ea***ms	to put emphasis on sth; to coin a memorable phrase
Onomatopoeia	the use of a word which imitates the sound it refers to	The cuckoo whizzed past the buzzing bees.	to evoke a feeling of sound, mood or movement
Foot	a group of stressed and unstressed syllables within a line of poetry which forms a metrical unit; the most important examples are:		In good poetry it is fused with the meaning: Different interpretations are often possible, e.g. a regular rhythm can be monotonous, but it might also stress the idea of peace and calm. Example: "Tomórrow, and tomórrow, and tomórrow créeps in this pétty páce from dáy to dáy" (Macbeth, V, 5) slow, monotonous → Macbeth feels that his life has lost all sense when he learns that his wife has died.
• iamb	sequence of unstressed/ stressed syllables	Bewáre … delíght	
• trochee	sequence of stressed/ unstressed syllables	Cómrades … ángels	
• anapaest	sequence of two unstressed/ one stressed syllables	Intervéne … undernéath	
• dactyl	sequence of one stressed/two unstressed syllables	Mérrily/háppily	

On the following pages you will have a look at a rather traditional poem. The terms above may help you to deal with it.

2.5 A traditional poem: Rhyme and rhythm

"Sonnet 18" is probably the most famous of Shakespeare's sonnets. Here are the first eight lines:

Traditional poetry: Shakespeare's "Sonnet 18"

Shall I compare thee to a summer's day?
Thou art more lovely and more temperate:
Rough winds do shake the darling buds of May,
And summer's lease hath all too short a date;
Sometimes too hot the eye of heaven shines,
And often is his gold complexion dimmed;
And every fair from fair sometimes declines,
By chance or nature's changing course untrimmed;

Margaret Ferguson et al. The Norton Anthology of Poetry. Fourth Edition. *New York, London: W. W. Norton&Company, 1996, p. 235.*

2 **temperate** mild, calm • 3 **darling buds** young, lovely flowers • 4 **lease** *(legal)* the right to use something for a certain time • 4 **date** *here:* duration • 5 **eye of heaven** *(fig.)* the sun • 6 **complexion** the natural skin colour • 7 **every fair** everything that is beautiful • 8 **nature's changing course untrimmed** the changing state of nature which is not controlled by anything

Now use your skills

a) *Having read the first eight lines of the poem, now determine the rhyme scheme.*

____

____

____

____

b) *Look at the following descriptions of metrical patterns. Which one illustrates the rhythm of the first line of Sonnet 18?*

a. \ – \ – \ – \ – \ –
b. – \ – \ – \ – \ – \
c. \ – – \ – – \ – – \

\ = stressed syllable
– = unstressed syllable

____

____

c) *Here are the last six lines of the sonnet but not in the correct order. Read the definition in the box and try to reconstruct the poem. The rhyme scheme will help you.*

Nor shall death brag thou wand'rest in his shade, ______________
So long lives this, and this gives life to thee. ______________
But thy eternal summer shall not fade, ______________
Nor lose possession of that fair thou ow'st; ______________
5 When in eternal lines to Time thou grow'st: ______________
So long as men can breathe, or eyes can see, ______________

William Shakespeare, "Sonnet 18" aus The Norton Anthology of Poetry. Margaret Ferguson et al. Fourth Edition. New York, London: W. W. Norton&Company, 1996

1 **to brag** to speak proudly of sth which may not be true • 2 **this** this sonnet • 4 **to owe** *(archaic)* to own • 5 **eternal lines** immortal verse • 5 **to time thou grow'st** you and time become one

Definition !

The English (Shakespearian) sonnet is usually written in three quatrains and a couplet rhyming **abab cdcd efef gg.** It often presents three arguments concerned with its theme in the three quatrains and draws a conclusion in the couplet.

2.6 A traditional poem: Content

The definition says that the sonnet often presents three arguments concerned with the theme in the three quatrains. In the couplet a conclusion is drawn.

a) *Examine "Sonnet 18" and note down the arguments and conclusion for the four stanzas.*

You have already looked at the rhymes and the rhythm in "Sonnet 18". Have a look at the imagery now. The first line already shows how important images are for this sonnet because the speaker asks himself "Shall I compare thee to a summer's day?" (l.1) but decides straight away that such a comparison would not be suitable: "Thou art more lovely and more temperate" (l.2).

b) *State all the metaphors and personifications you find in the sonnet. Which areas of life are they taken from?*

c) *"Sonnet 18" is the most famous of Shakespeare's sonnets. Although it is 400 years old, lots of people know it by heart because they studied it at school. No course on Shakespeare seems to be complete without it. Explain why. Refer to the content and the form.*

3 Drama

3.1 Getting started: The nature of drama

Tip !

drama = <u>any</u> work meant to be performed on a stage i.e. comedy, tragedy, tragicomedy etc.

Dramatic texts are very different from short stories or poems because, unlike stories and poems, they are <u>not</u> written to be read but to be **performed** and, to look at it from the **audience's** point of view, **watched**. Outside school or university, people do not normally sit down to read a play, unless they are planning a trip to the theatre. But even then they are more likely to consult a plot summary or maybe read a **review** from a newspaper or magazine rather than read the script of the play. Studying a dramatic text is like looking at the score of a symphony: Unless you are very musical, it is hard to imagine what the music would sound like.

When a **playwright** or **dramatist** sits down to put pen to paper, he has **directors**, **stage managers** and **actresses/actors** in mind. This is why a dramatic text usually consists of two parts: **dialogue** and **stage directions**. In a play, **dialogue** covers all the spoken language, not only the conversation of two characters as the word might suggest. The **stage directions** give information about how to perform the play. This might refer to the setting, scenery, the characters' movements, tone of voice etc.

a) *Think about the differences between novels and plays. Look at the following statements and arrange them into two groups depending on whether they refer to <u>novelists</u> or rather to <u>dramatists</u>.*

can set the action of his story wherever he likes • will often set the action in an ordinary room in a private house • has to work with only a limited number of characters • can follow the activities of his characters over long periods of time • must limit the action to what can be shown in three hours or less • may have to use messenger reports or eye-witness accounts • can allow the reader access to the characters' minds

Novelist	Dramatist
✎	✎
✎	✎
✎	✎
	✎

Now use your skills

b) *With the help of the **Useful phrases** below and with what you have found out so far write a short paragraph about the nature of drama.*

Useful phrases !

Drama	is limited is restricted	with regard to with reference to	setting changes of scene portrayal of spectacular actions, e.g. violence actions which span long periods of time
The dramatist/ playwright	will often try to may have to	simplify things to a certain extent restrict the scope of the action concentrate the action to cover a short period of time	

On the following pages you will deal with a modern play first. After that you will look at a classic traditional play by William Shakespeare. The things you learn apply to both – traditional and modern drama.

Tip !

"Pravda" is called "A Fleet Street Comedy". "Fleet Street", which is near St Paul's Cathedral in London, used to be the home of British national newspapers. Today most have moved their headquarters to the Docklands.

A modern play: Howard Brenton/David Hare: *Pravda. A Fleet Street Comedy*

The play shows how Lambert Le Roux, a modern press baron, conquers Fleet Street journalism. Andrew May is a young journalist working for the Leicester Bystander, a provincial newspaper. Shortly after the end of this excerpt he learns that the paper has been bought by Le Roux.

Scene Two

NEWSVENDORS, *carrying newspapers, come on. They deliver headlines.*

FIRST NEWSVENDOR. HEADLESS MURDER CASE: WHOSE HEAD IS IT?

SECOND. SEX TUTOR SAYS 'SHE LOVED ME'.

THIRD. TWELVE GO-GO DANCERS FOUND IN CRATE AT HEATHROW: TWELVE EXCLUSIVES.

FIRST. ARAB LOVE NEST HORROR. TWENTY-TWO HELD.

SECOND. ROYAL HAIR-DO. CUT OUT AND KEEP.

THIRD. GAY BISHOP. MP's PROTEST.

Meanwhile a female film star is pursued across the stage by reporters.

REPORTERS. Cindy! Cindy! Look at me. What about his wife?

CINDY. No comment.

REPORTERS. Cindy, Cindy come on give us something – Cindy it's our living.

CINDY. I just have this to say. Mr Ramero and I just love the Caribbean. There is nothing between us. The President of Uruguay is just a fun person.

Two REPORTERS *come forward, each with a notebook and a telephone crooked between shoulder and neck.*

FIRST REPORTER. The accused – two Cs – said that Jayne – that's a-y-n-e Jephcott – that's ph ... double 't' – had invited him windsurfing and that afterwards they had sex – that's s-e-x if you're wondering ...

SECOND. The murder weapon, an open and bloodstained baked bean can, was found embedded in the victim's neck. Stop para ...

FIRST. ... on the sand under the soggy – that's two 'g's sail – that's s-a-i-l. The defendant, that's twenty-seven year-old Alberto Santin. I am a born-again Christian ...

SECOND. No I haven't actually got an interview but if I had an interview it would go 'interviewed today at her Colchester home the accused's wife said, "I walked into the kitchen and I noticed that he was in an unusual posture. When I investigated further a metal object ..."'

Meanwhile ANDREW *comes forward and addresses us directly.*

ANDREW. I love it. The smell of hot type. The thunder of the foundry. The nightly rush for the first edition. Oh God I love it so. The romance. All my career. The world passing through a newsroom. Processed, bundled and delivered through your door.

Howard Brenton/David Hare. Pravda. A Fleet Street Comedy. A Methuen Modern Play. London: Methuen, 1986.

1 **newsvendor** a person who sells newspapers, usually outside on the streets • 4 **Heathrow** London's largest international airport • 5 **exclusive** a story about famous people which is published in only one newspaper or magazine • 7 **hair-do** style in which a woman's hair is arranged • 25 **born-again** having come to have a strong belief in a particular religion and wanting other people to have the same belief • 25 **Colchester** town in East Anglia • 31 **foundry** a factory where metal or glass is melted and made into different shapes and objects

3.2 A modern play: Setting, action, atmosphere

Despite all the differences mentioned so far, dramatic texts and narrative texts have some things in common, too. For analysing plays or an excerpt from a play, it is as important to look at the **setting**, the **action** and the **characters** as it is for narrative texts. (→ see pp.29–34)

Now use your skills

a) *Read the excerpt from* Pravda. *Note down the information you get about the …*

Setting: ______________________________

____

Action: ______________________________

____

____

Characters: ______________________________

____

Having discussed the terms above, you can now turn to the **atmosphere** of the play.

b) *Choose the most suitable adjectives from below to describe the atmosphere (the emotional mood) that is evoked in this scene.*

hectic • friendly • tragic • feverish • restless • desperate • confusing • exciting • tumultuous

____

____

____

____

____

Tip !
It can be a help to imagine watching the play on stage. What would be your impression?

3.3 A modern play: Characters

Let's have a closer look at the **characters** and **characterisation** in *Pravda*. You are already familiar with the terms **'direct'** and **'indirect' characterisation** (sometimes the terms 'explicit' and 'implicit' are used). Can a playwright use these techniques, too? What are the specific problems he is confronted with?

a) *Have a look at the following list of things a playwright can do to inform the reader/audience about his characters. Copy the grid in your exercise book and fill in the things from the list.*

- what the character does/how he or she behaves towards other characters
- what other characters say about him/her
- what the character says about himself/herself
- the way in which the character talks (e.g. choice of words, dialect, quality of voice)
- description of the character's outward appearance in the stage directions (e.g. age, clothes)
- special sound effects/lighting to accompany the character's entrances/exits
- description of the character's facial expressions or gestures in the stage directions
- what the character actually says (ideas, opinions, values he/she expresses in his/her utterances)

Direct/explicit	**Indirect/implicit**
what other characters say about him/her …	the way in which the character talks (e.g. choice of words, dialect, quality of voice) …

b) *Now look at the two columns. What problems do they reveal for you as a reader?*

Now use your skills

c) *Collect all the information we get about the characters in the excerpt from* Pravda *in the table below. Then explain what conclusions we can draw from it.*

Character	Information	Conclusion
newsvendors	no names, just numbers (e.g. l.2, l.5) read out headlines dealing with sex, crime, celebrities (ll.2–8)	not presented as individuals, just representatives of a group no individual utterances, act as mouthpieces of the press
reporters	✎	✎
Cindy	✎	✎
Andrew	✎	✎

3.4 A modern play: Elements of comedy

Pravda is classified as a **comedy**.

a) *Study the following definition carefully.*

Definition !

A **comedy** is a type of drama which deals with a light topic or with a serious topic in an amusing way. It has a happy ending and usually makes fun of what is ridiculous or absurd. The central characters are ordinary people. Other characters very often just personify certain **types** or **characters** of little individuality. Comedy evokes laughter or amusement and, at its best, makes us think.

Now use your skills

b) *Read the excerpt from* Pravda *once more. Which of the characteristics of comedy can you find in this excerpt?*

When talking about comedies, one should also deal with **humour**. It is not easy to explain how humour is created. And very often an explanation destroys the effect. Furthermore, different people laugh about different things, i.e. it is a very subjective experience. Nevertheless, it is important for you to be familiar with the most important devices that help to create humour. Amusing or funny effects can basically be achieved in two ways: words or actions.

Humour based on actions		**Humour based on words**	
Slapstick/horseplay/ knockabout entertainment	The humour is based on simple actions, e.g. people hitting each other, falling down. It involves people acting in a deliberately silly way in order to make the audience laugh. You find this kind of humour in silent movies but also in most films starring Rowan Atkinson.	**Hyperbole**	an overstatement, an exaggeration used to emphasise a particular feeling
		Pun	a play on words in which one word has two different meanings, e.g. Big cuts at hospital
		Joke	A joke is something funny that is said. Very often it is a story and its last words make it funny. These words are called the **punch line**.
Practical joke/prank	A trick that is played on people to make them look stupid and to make other people laugh, e.g. tricks played on April Fool's Day, tricks played in the famous TV show *Candid Camera*.	**(Verbal) Irony**	the use of words to express the opposite of the words' literal meaning
		Satire	a humorous way of criticising people to show their faults or weaknesses
Dramatic Irony situations in which a character's words have a different meaning for the audience because they have some information the character does not have			
Parody an imitation of the style of something (piece of writing, music, acting) in order to be amusing			

Useful phrases !	
Comedy	• makes fun of all kinds of foolish behaviour and absurdity. • shows life as good and worth living. • relies on stock characters (types or stereotypes). • features misunderstandings, mistaken identity, surprises, discoveries. • often uses highly artificial means of plot resolution.
The scene The text	• is full of humour. • is written in a humorous tone.
The action	• is funny because there is a lot of slapstick/horseplay. • makes us laugh because there are a lot of practical jokes/pranks.
The humour	• originates from the contrast between … • springs from the use of puns, jokes, irony, satire, parody, hyperbole.
The irony The sarcasm	• is directed against an institution. • attacks human foolishness. • ridicules a certain idea. • exposes people's stupidity. • makes fun of … .

Now use your skills

c) *Examine how humour is created in the excerpt from* Pravda. *Complete the following table:*

Example	**Device**	**Classification + explanation** **based on action**	**based on words**
"HEADLESS MURDER CASE: WHOSE HEAD IS IT?" **(l.2)**	parody		→ imitates the style of headlines in popular papers
"Meanwhile a female film star is pursued across the stage by reporters." **(l.9)**	parody	✎	
	hyperbole		→ exaggerated use of spelling
"TWELVE GO-GO DANCERS FOUND IN CRATE AT HEATHROW: TWELVE EXCLUSIVES" **(ll.4–5)**	✎		→ creates an unintended funny effect because of the paradox (twelve – exclusives)
"I love it. The smell of hot type […] through your door." **(ll.31–33)**	(form of) dramatic irony	✎	

3.5 A traditional play: Communication and images

Now look at a more traditional play. In contrast to the dialogue in the excerpt from *Pravda* the dialogue between Romeo and Juliet below is an example of meaningful communication, i.e. both characters are genuinely interested in each other and this is the message they want to get across.

A traditional play: William Shakespeare: *Romeo and Juliet*

Act I, Scene 5, ll.92–118
The play is set in Verona. For many years there has been a bitter quarrel between two important families, the Capulets and the Montagues. Whenever members of the two families meet, they fight. Romeo and Juliet are the children of these two families.

The scene shows their first meeting at a dance at the Capulets' house. They are not formally introduced; they don't know each other's names. Romeo has come to the dance in disguise because he hopes to see Rosaline, the woman he thinks he is in love with. But when he sees Juliet he falls head over heels in love with her.

Romeo *[To Juliet]* If I profane with my unworthiest hand
This holy shrine, the gentle sin is this:
My lips, two blushing pilgrims, ready stand
To smooth that rough touch with a tender kiss.

Juliet Good pilgrim, you do wrong your hand too much,
Which mannerly devotion shows in this;
For saints have hands that pilgrims' hands do touch,
And palm to palm is holy palmers' kiss.

Romeo Have not saints lips, and holy palmers too?

Juliet Ay, pilgrim, lips that they must use in prayer.

Romeo O then, dear saint, let lips do what hands do:
They pray: grant thou, lest faith turn to despair.

Juliet Saints do not move, though grant for prayers' sake.

Romeo Then move not, while my prayer's effect I take.
[He kisses her.]
Thus from my lips, by thine my sin is purg'd.

Juliet Then have my lips the sin that they have took.

Romeo Sin from my lips? O trespass sweetly urg'd!
Give me my sin again.

Juliet You kiss by th' book.

Nurse Madam, your mother craves a word with you.

Romeo What is her mother?

Nurse Marry, bachelor,
Her mother is the lady of the house,
And a good lady, and a wise and virtuous:
I nurs'd her daughter that you talk'd withal.
I tell you, he that can lay hold of her
Shall have the chinks.

Romeo Is she a Capulet?
O dear account. My life is my foe's debt.

Benvolio Away, be gone; the sport is at the best.

William Shakespeare: "Romeo and Juliet": Act I, Scene 5, ll.92–118. From: Brian Gibbons (ed.). The Arden Edition of the Works of William Shakespeare: Romeo and Juliet, Methuen, London and New York, 1980.

1 **to profane** to be disrespectful • 2 **this holy shrine** i.e. Juliet's hand • 6 **mannerly devotion** proper respect • 8 **palm** the inner surface of the hand •8 **palmer** pilgrims to Jerusalem who brought back palm leaves • 12 **to grant** *here:* to give in • 12 **lest** so that not • 14 **prayer's effect** result of his prayer *(i.e. a kiss)* • 16 **to purge** to make sth or sb pure • 18 **trespass** entering another person's property without permission; *here:* sin • 20 **by the book** expertly • 21 **to crave** to ask for sth • 23 **Marry** by the Virgin Mary • 23 **bachelor** unmarried gentleman • 26 **withal** with • 28 **the chinks** plenty of money • 30 **foe** enemy • 31 **Benvolio** Romeo's friend

Now use your skills

a) *Examine Romeo and Juliet's dialogue carefully. There is a sonnet 'hidden' in their dialogue. Find the beginning and the end.*

b) *Count the number of lines they each deliver. How are they distributed so that they form a sonnet?*

c) *Explain why the third quatrain and the couplet illustrate that Romeo and Juliet are a perfect match.*

d) *Analyse the imagery that is used: Look at the terms Romeo and Juliet use to address each other. Explain where they come from and what you associate with them. A dictionary can help you.*

e) *Find more words/phrases that are taken from the same sphere. The annotations might help you.*

3.6 A traditional play: Stage directions

What makes the scene hard to understand – apart from the language – is the almost complete **absence of stage directions**. This is fairly common in Shakespeare's plays. His notes on how to perform the dramatic text are usually restricted to basic instructions like **'enter'** or **'exit'**. In this part of the scene even those are missing.

a) *Read the text again carefully and suggest where those basic stage directions might be added.*

b) *Examine the sonnet again and give further, more specific stage directions.*

Definition !

One stage direction often found in Shakespeare's plays is **aside**. The **aside** is a device in which a character breaks the fourth wall and addresses a few words to the audience only. By convention, the other characters on the stage cannot hear these words.

Another dramatic convention which was often used in Elizabethan plays is the **soliloquy**. The **soliloquy** is a speech in which a character is alone on the stage and reveals his thoughts and feelings to the audience. Hamlet's "To be or not to be" is a famous example. Since the beginning of realistic drama, these two conventions have practically disappeared.

3.7 A traditional play: Approaches to tragedy

This excerpt from the play is, of course, very romantic. But even at this early stage there is a sense of foreboding. The lovers are not left to live in a fool's paradise for long.

a) *Find the clue.*

Below you find a box with some information about tragedy. Even at this early stage of the play you can define *Romeo and Juliet* as a tragedy.

b) *Read the definition in the box and note down what makes* Romeo and Juliet *a tragedy at this early stage.*

Definition !

A **tragedy** is a type of drama in which the protagonist passes through a series of misfortunes towards his downfall. An essential element in the definition of tragedy is the character of the **tragic hero**. In traditional tragedy the **tragic hero** is neither too good nor too bad and his ruin is brought about by some **error of judgement or a tragic flaw** in his character.

Already in this early scene of the play the reader gets the feeling …

Of course dealing with an extract of a tragedy is not enough to get a general understanding of tragedy. Nevertheless, these approaches can give you a general idea. Of course at school you will discuss literature in more detail.

Having dealt with written texts so far, you will now shift your attention to visual texts.

Text analysis: D Visual texts

Maybe you ask yourself: What is a visual text? Aren't texts made up of words, sentences, paragraphs etc.? As this chapter will show, visuals can be seen as texts, too, and can be analysed along similar lines.

A written text transports a meaning and uses certain elements to do so. Pictures and other visuals do exactly the same; they just don't use words for it. Your task when analysing a written text is to find out which meaning is transported by which elements (e.g. by saying which functions the stylistic devices in a text have). In this chapter you will learn to identify the visual elements for getting a message across and you will practise how to put your findings into words.

1 Pictures

1.1 Getting started: Four-step analysis

All kinds of pictures, from oil paintings to pencil sketches, can be analysed using the following four steps. They will help you to deal with a picture systematically, so that no important aspect is left out. You will find more detailed information about how to apply these steps to specific types of pictures on the next few pages.

Useful phrases: Describing positions !

in the middle/centre
at the top/bottom
on the left/right
in the top right-hand corner
in the bottom left-hand corner
in the background/foreground

Step 1: Introduction – basic information
Your introduction should answer the following questions:
- Where is the image from? Who made it and when?
- What type of image is it?
- What does the image (roughly) show?
- Why was it drawn/taken?

Step 2: Description
Look at the picture carefully, then describe it systematically, e.g.:
- from the centre to the corners
- from the foreground to the background
- from the left to the right (or the other way round)
- from the top to the bottom (or the other way round)

Don't forget to look at details:
- the setting (place and time) and/or the situation
- the quality of the picture (clear or blurred, realistic or abstract, etc.)
- the striking features of the objects
- the characters, e.g. their appearance and body language (facial expressions, gestures, postures)

Tip !

When describing what people are doing in a picture, always use the **present progressive**: The woman on the left **is entering** a shop.

Step 3: Analysis
- Does the image transport a message/have an intended effect?
- Which pictorial elements are used to get the message across/to produce the effect?
- How do the different elements interact?

Step 4: Evaluation
- Do you think that the image is effective in getting the message to the target group?
- Does it use suitable means for doing so?
- What effect does the image have on you?

1.2 Photographs, paintings and drawings

Pictures include drawings, paintings and photographs, but of course each of these categories can be specified further:

drawings	pencil/charcoal/ink drawing; portrait, caricature, cartoon, …
paintings	watercolour/oil painting; portrait, landscape painting, still-life, …
photographs	black and white/colour photograph, …

Now use your skills

a) *Have a look at the photograph below and then fill in the gaps in the sentences which describe and analyse it. If you need help, look at the **Useful phrases** next to the picture.*

Useful phrases: Describing pictures !

- The picture shows/depicts/sends an indirect message/captures a key moment/makes an appeal …
- It conveys the impression that …
- An element of the photo has the effect that …/ indicates or represents sth/is a sign that …
- The photographer aims to present …/creates an atmosphere of …
- The photo appeals/does not appeal to me.
- In my opinion, the picture is effective/ convincing/…
- All pictorial elements support …/contribute to …
- The photo touches me/leaves me cold because …
- It visually describes …/makes a problem visible.

The photo __shows__ a man begging on the pavement and another man passing by. ____________ the beggar, there are a reddish cup and a cardboard sign which states that ________________________. The homeless man is hiding his face and the passer-by's head is cut off by the ________________, therefore both are ____________.

There is a clear ____________ between light and shadow, which cuts the picture roughly into two halves, ____________ from the bottom left ____________ corner. The dark half is slightly larger, but there is a red strip of brick wall cutting through it ____________.

The homeless man ____________ in the dark half near the centre and is wearing black clothes which merge with the dark ____________. Only his cardboard sign and the cup are bright. The other man ____________ red shoes and bright blue jeans. He is walking in the sun around the homeless person, his hands in his pockets.

The two ____________ of the picture ____________ two different worlds: the dark one of the homeless, and the bright and colourful normal one. The homeless man belongs entirely to the dark half; only his cup and cardboard sign asking for help are intruding into colourful life. The passer-by is avoiding them, which ____________ that he does not realise the other's problems or does not care. However, the bright red strip of brick wall ____________ into the dark half and might represent the hope that it is possible to ________________________.

The ____________ of the photographer is probably an ____________ to show more compassion with people who live outside mainstream society, and also to reflect on ________________________.

b) *Do you think the photograph is an effective appeal for helping homeless people? Give reasons for your opinion.*

____

____

____

____

Tip !

'Cartoon' can also mean a series of drawings inside boxes that tell a (short) story (= comic strip), or a short animated film, such as "Tom and Jerry".

1.3 Cartoons

A cartoon is a humorous drawing that critically deals with a current news item, i.e. it responds to a topical event. It often contains some text, e.g. speech/thought/sound bubbles and/or a caption (text under the picture).

A cartoon is critical of people or institutions in the news, topical events or new trends/ideas (its *target*) and usually makes a one-sided point (its *message*). It usually combines visual techniques (e.g. caricaturing a person or using objects with a symbolic meaning) with verbal humour (wordplay, irony …) (its *devices*).

Of course the four-step analysis can be applied to cartoons, too. Look at the cartoon below and do exercises a) to d), which represent one step each.

Now use your skills

a) *Step 1 (Introduction): The grid below contains the questions your introduction has to cover. Fill it in and then turn your notes into a paragraph.*

Useful phrases: Introducing cartoons !

The cartoon
- was drawn by [name of cartoonist].
- was published/appeared in [newspaper] on [date].
- was created in response to [a news item].
- shows/presents/depicts/deals with/alludes to/ refers to/criticises [an event/crisis/trend/…].
- is directed at/comments on/targets [an attitude, policy …].

Where is the picture from?	✎
Who made it and when?	✎
What type of picture is it?	✎
What does it (roughly) show?	✎

b) *Step 2 (Description): Now describe the cartoon in a short paragraph. If you need help, look at the* ***Useful phrases*** *to the left or the position vocabulary on page 56.*

Useful phrases: Describing cartoons !

The cartoon
- consists of/is made up of … several pictorial elements/speech or thought bubbles/a caption.
- is divided into …

The caption
- is a comment/statement by …
- states that …/reinforces the cartoonist's message that …
- is unexpected/short and sweet/ironic.

c) *Step 3 (Analysis): Examine the elements in their relationships and functions. What message do they convey? Pay special attention to the characters!*

Useful phrases: Analysing cartoons !

The cartoon expresses sth/points out that …
An element in the drawing represents/stands for/symbolises…/is exaggerated/stressed.
A character is a caricature of …/the stereotypical …
A character is caricatured/ridiculed as …
The humour lies in the difference/misunderstanding/discrepancy/contrast/parallels between … and …
The message of the cartoon is obvious/clear: It aims to show that …
The key point the cartoon is trying to make is to expose the fact that …
The cartoonist criticises … for doing sth/makes fun of …

d) *Step 4 (Evaluation): Do you agree with this evaluation of the cartoon? Discuss.*

Possible student's answer:
The cartoon only partly achieves its aim. It remains unclear if it aims to praise the Harry Potter novels' ability to fascinate the young generation, or if it criticises the media habits of the middle-aged generation. If I do not recognise the message of a cartoon at once, its point is lost on me. Yet it is clear that, according to the cartoon, both generations live in different media worlds side by side without contact. The cartoonist skilfully presents this contrast by dividing the cartoon into two halves. Some may call this simplistic, but this device works for me in presenting the differences between parents and children.

Useful phrases: Evaluating cartoons !

The cartoon achieves its aim of [doing sth]. It skilfully/effectively …
The point/message of the cartoon is lost on me/fails to work for me because …
The cartoon appeals/does not appeal to me. In my opinion it is
- detailed/well-made/very clever/effective/of high quality/convincing …
- simplistic/confusing/unfair/exaggerated/…

2 Tables, graphs and charts

2.1 Getting started: Definitions

If information consists of numbers, it can be visualised in different ways. For each of these ways it is important to keep the following questions in mind:

- When looking at numbers, always check their source: Are the numbers reliable, trustworthy and up-to-date?
- Why are the numbers presented in this form, e.g. as a table or a chart? Think of the different functions of visualisations (see overview below).
- Is the visualisation accurate? The units of measurement on the two axes should not be manipulated.
- If conclusions are drawn: Are they really supported by the numbers? Are there other possible interpretations?

Here are examples of the four most common visualisations together with their names. Read the definitions and functions in the grid below and then fill in the correct visualisations and their names.

Visualisations:

1

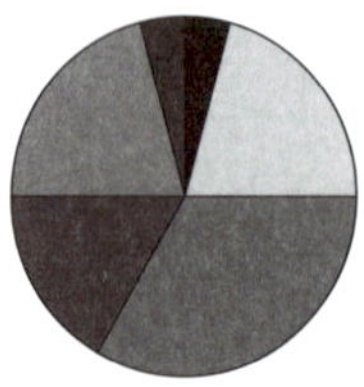

2

2012	2016	2020
13	15	18
22	25	26

3

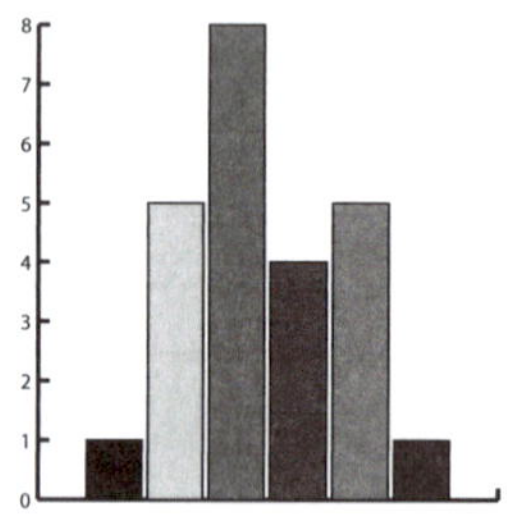

4

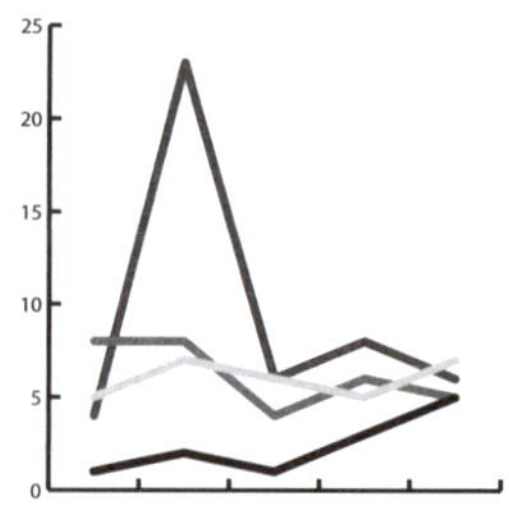

Names:

pie chart

(line) graph

table

bar chart

Visualisation	Name	Definition	Function
		• a grid with numbers systematically arranged in lines and columns	• gives **raw data** as a basis for analysis
		• one or more lines in a system of coordinates with two axes – a horizontal and a vertical one	• shows the **development** of sth over a period of time (tendencies and trends)
		• boxes of different height/length in a system of coordinates with two axes – a horizontal and a vertical one	• shows **differences** between various things
		• circle divided into different sections	• shows the **percentages** of a whole

2.2 Tables

When dealing with tables (as well as graphs and charts), the four-step analysis you have practised with pictures is useful again. However, you will need different vocabulary to put the numbers, lines and percentages into words, especially for steps 1 and 2: Introduction and description.

Ferguson traffic stops, 2013: Population stopped by the police, total	
	drivers stopped in total
black	ca. 86%
white	ca. 14%

Ferguson traffic stops, 2013: Reasons for being stopped by the police			
	Breaking a traffic law	**License or equipment problem**	**Investigative (e.g. searching for a suspect)**
black	**43%**	**58%**	**7%**
white or other	**68%**	**32%**	**4%**

Source: Office of the Missouri Attorney General (2014). Racial Profiling Data/2013: Ferguson Police Department.
Note: Because data are based on stops and not drivers, drivers with multiple stops are counted multiple times. Reasons for stops exceed 100% because some stops were made for multiple reasons.

Now use your skills

a) *Look at the tables above and answer the six introduction questions in the grid.*

Introduction	
What is its **topic**?	number of drivers controlled by ______________ and ______________ of the people stopped
What type of **presentation** has been chosen? (→ see p.60)	two ______________
What is its **source**? (a newspaper, a survey of an organisation, state department, etc.)	______________
What is its **time of publication**?	______________
What **period of time** is covered or what **point of time** does it refer to?	______________
What **figures** are presented – numbers (e.g. 456) or percentage figures (e.g. 26.8%)?	______________ figures

b) *Describe the tables "Ferguson traffic stops, 2013" focusing on the amount of people stopped by the police and their ethnicity. Turn each percentage figure into words and write them into the grid, using the expressions in the box.*

The vast majority of drivers controlled by the police are black. / More white than black drivers are controlled by the police.	stopped in total
	stopped because of breaking a traffic law
	stopped because of license or equipment problems
	stopped for investigative reasons

Useful phrases: Talking about numbers !

- Almost no …
- Only very few …
- A tiny minority of …
- Less than …
- Roughly one out of four …
- A third of the …
- Exactly two out of five …
- Half of the …
- Over two thirds of …
- More than …
- A high percentage of …
- The overwhelming/vast majority …
- Most …
- More X than Y …
- Twice as many …

c) *Comment on the problem of mistrust between the police and Afro-Americans and how to overcome it. Refer to information provided in the table "Ferguson traffic stops, 2013" and in the text "Can familiarity build trust …" on p. 9.* (writing a comment → pp.71–75)

2.3 Graphs

a) *For describing graphs, you need to be able to put lines into words. Read the phrases below carefully and look up those which you do not know.*

Useful phrases: Talking about changes and extremes !

to reach	a peak a low point	in the year … of more than five million
	an all-time high/low of …	
to go through a period of steady growth to remain constant to experience a sudden reversal		
a sudden/unexpected a slight/barely noticeable a steep/sharp/rapid a gradual/steady/continual	fall/drop decrease/decline increase/rise/growth	of 5% to 200 euros in temperature
		took place from … to … occurred in the year …
to go up/to grow to increase/to rise to decrease/to fall/to drop	unexpectedly/sharply gradually/steadily continually /consistently	by 2% at a certain rate

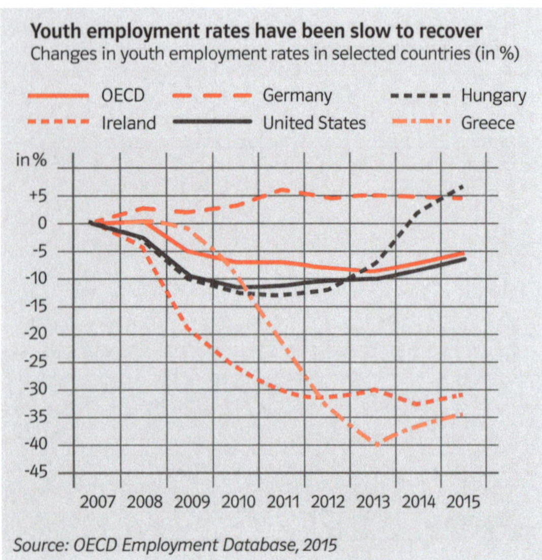

Now use your skills

b) *Have a close look at the line graph to the left. Fill in the gaps in the following text, which answers the six introduction questions from the page before.*

The title of the line graph on the right is ______________________________

____.

It refers to its topic, i.e. the effect of the Great Recession of the late 2000s and early 2010s on jobs for ____________ people in ____________. The graph was published by the ____________ in ____________ . ____________ lines in a single system of coordinates, one for each country, cover the period from ________ to ________ . The figures presented on the ________ axis are the ____________ of the change in youth employment starting from the base point in 2007.

c) *Study the lines in "Youth employment rates have been slow to recover" in detail. Add the missing countries and the descriptions in the grid below.*

Development	Youth employment in
From 2010 to 2012, the youth employment in this country sharply decreased until it reached its lowest point in 2013.	
	Ireland
Since 2013, the youth employment rate in this country has steadily increased.	
	United States

2.4 Charts

Charts can be either pie charts or bar charts. Both are ideal to visualise the relation between different numbers. Pie charts always represent percentages (with the whole "pie" being 100 %); bar charts can also represent absolute numbers, like the one in b) below. You will find that many of the phrases above, particularly **Useful phrases: Talking about numbers** (→ see p.61), can be applied to charts, too.

Now use your skills

a) *Look at the pie chart on the right. It is taken from the Pew Research Center study about the religious composition of international migrants. Describe it with the help of the* ***Useful phrases*** *in the box on the right.*

Useful phrases: Pie charts !

- The pie chart shows/reveals how … is divided/ made up of …
- The whole circle stands for …
- The pie is subdivided into … segments which represent the …
- The share of … of the total … is about 20 per cent.
- The biggest/smallest section …

Religious Composition of International Migrants

Percentage and estimated number of all migrants who belong to each religious group

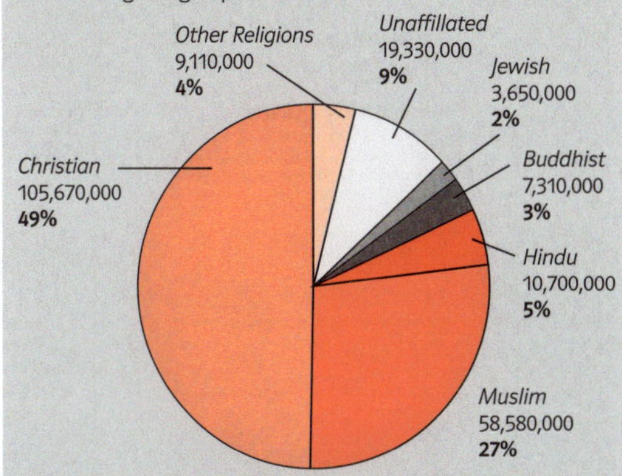

Pew Research Center's Forum on Religion & Public Life Global Religion and Migration Database 2010

b) *Now look at the bar chart on the right and read the* ***Useful phrases*** *below. Compare the countries in a short paragraph.*

The countries with the best and worst annual salaries for teachers

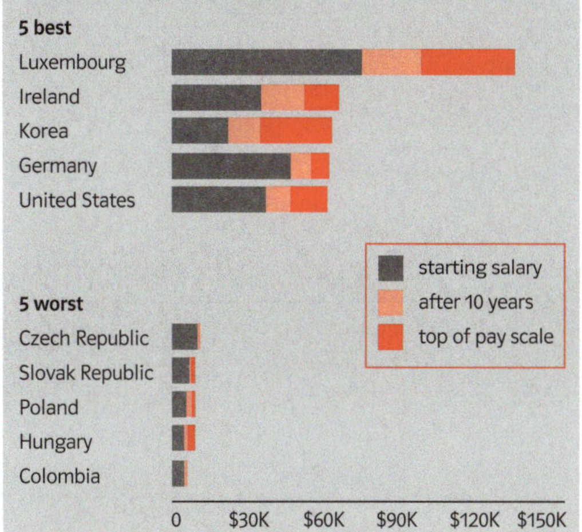

Source: OECD, 2015

Useful phrases: Bar charts !

- highest/lowest figure/score
- no/little difference between X and Y
- to be at the top/bottom of the ranking
- to achieve an average/below-average/above-average figure
- in comparison with/in contrast to

c) *Below there are suggestions about if and how you could present the information from "Youth employment rates" in other ways. Think about the advantages or disadvantages of each type of visual and fill in the empty boxes in the grid.*

"Youth employment rates" as a . . .				
	table	**line graph**	**pie chart**	**bar chart**
Possible?	yes	only with additional figures over a period of time; the different countries could be represented by lines in different colours	no, you would need to add up all of the teacher salaries in the world (or continent, as long as it is a whole) and show what percentage each country's teachers make	yes
Advantages/ disadvantages	can include more raw information than the others; exact; visually boring	✎	✎	✎

Text analysis: E Audiovisual texts

1 Audiovisual texts

Analysing films is not so different from analysing written texts. Some things apply to both: You look at the setting, the characters or the storyline in general, for example. However, you need new tools and terms, too, which you will find on the following pages.

1.1 Getting started: Camera operations

For an audiovisual text, the different camera operations fulfil a similar role as the narrator in prose texts: They determine what the reader/viewer knows and influence his/her perception. Therefore, it is essential to be able to identify and name these operations in order to analyse a film.

a) *Match the definitions for field size or camera movements below with the correct picture. Then learn the definitions, e.g. by using the common "cover up and memorise" technique.*

long shot: people/objects shown from a distance **extreme close-up:** e.g. face only, or a detailed shot of an object **full shot:** shot of the whole body/object **close-up:** e.g. head and shoulders **medium shot:** upper body, part of an object	
Field size	

crane shot: camera moves flexibly in all directions on a crane **static shot:** camera does not move **tracking shot:** camera is on a vehicle moving on the ground **to pan left/right; to tilt up/down** **to zoom in on/out of sth** (e.g. a face)	
Camera movements	

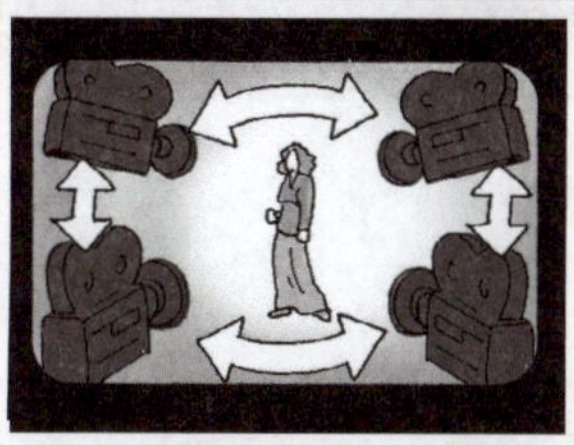	

b) *In the following grid, the definitions at the top describe camera positions and angles. Match them with the correct picture. When you know the terms, move on to the next page to work on their functions.*

eye-level shot: depending on the filmed person's eye-level
establishing shot: shows location at the start of a scene, e.g. by a long shot and a slow pan
low-angle shot: from below
overhead shot: bird's eye view
reverse-angle shot: from the opposite side, usually shows a dialogue partner
high-angle shot: from above
over-the-shoulder shot: from behind

Camera positions	

Camera angles	

1.2 Camera operations: Function

What functions can the different camera operations have? Complete the grids below with the phrases next to them. Feel free to add other possible functions you can think of.

Distance between the camera and the object

Field size	Function
long shot	*presents a larger picture for orientation*
full shot	✎
medium shot	✎
close-up	✎
extreme close-up	✎

- ~~presents a larger picture for orientation~~
- draws viewers' attention to sb or sth special, e.g. reveals sb's feelings by showing his/her facial expression
- gives particular attention to a detail from a very short distance to show its importance in a scene
- gives a complete picture of sb or sth
- brings viewers closer to a person/an action

Position and angle of the camera

Type of shot	Function
establishing shot	gives an overview of the location in preparation for the following action
✎	gives an impression of the action/setting below from an unusual perspective
✎	viewers feel involved in the dialogue
✎	used after the over-the-shoulder shot to give viewers the perspective of the other dialogue partner
✎	an unusual perspective from a higher position, which makes a character seem small and weak
✎	the usual horizontal perspective, often unnoticed by the viewer; no special function
✎	an unusual perspective from a lower position: enlarges sth and stresses its importance/power

- high-angle shot
- eye-level shot
- overhead shot
- low-angle shot
- ~~establishing shot~~
- over-the-shoulder shot
- reverse-angle shot

Camera movement

Camera movement	Function
static shot	*can give an impression of calmness*
to pan left/right	✎
to tilt up/down	✎
to zoom in on/out of sth	✎
crane shot	✎
tracking shot	✎
hand-held camera	✎

- allows viewers to follow an action closely at eye-level; may add speed to a scene
- shows an object or person in full length
- the abrupt, unsteady movements create an impression of reality/authenticity
- ~~can give an impression of calmness~~
- concentrates attention on or moves attention away from sb or sth
- gives a wider impression of a location; may follow an action or show different characters
- a very flexible shot from different positions with smooth transitions

1.3 Interpreting body language

a) *A film offers the chance to characterise someone indirectly through his/her body language. What emotions, attitudes or messages does the following body language usually show? Sometimes more than one solution is possible, depending on the situation. Add the adjectives, too. Feel free to use a dictionary if necessary.*

Choice of nouns:

- interest
- disappointment
- vanity
- indecision
- frustration
- happiness
- ~~impatience~~
- attention
- insecurity
- ~~nervousness~~
- disinterest
- stress

Body language	**POSSIBLE INTERPRETATION** **nouns**	 **adjectives**
tapping or drumming your fingers	nervousness impatience	nervous impatient
biting your nails	✎	✎
having your head tilted	✎	✎
stroking your chin	✎	✎
looking down, your face turned away from your partner	✎	✎
patting your hair	✎	✎
smiling brightly	✎	✎

b) *Now work the other way round: Think of situations in which body language expresses the corresponding emotions in the left-hand column and fill them in.*

Emotions (noun/adjective)	**Body language**
attention/attentive interest/interested understanding/understanding	keeping eye contact and nodding when listening in a dialogue
anger/angry	standing with your hands on your hips
boredom/bored	✎
authority/authoritative confidence/confident	✎
depression/depressed	✎
scepticism/sceptical doubt/doubtful	✎
tiredness/tired	✎
disbelief/disbelieving expectation/expectant	✎
aggression/aggressive	✎
delight/delighted	✎
relaxation/relaxed	✎
defensiveness/defensive rejection/rejecting	✎

1.4 The four steps of film scene analysis

When viewing a film scene three times, you may follow this step-by-step approach.
See the next page for a model note-taking sheet.

Step 1: First viewing – focus on action	
→ Try to understand the gist of the action, including key phrases of the dialogue.	
Focus on action	
setting	What is the time and place of the action? What atmosphere is created?
plot	What happens and why?
suspense	Which questions remain unanswered? Why do you want to keep on viewing?

Step 2: Second viewing – focus on characters
→ Describe first, and then comment on the impressions conveyed by the character(s).
Focus on characters
appearance: hair – cleanliness – clothes
body language: face – gestures – posture – movements
language/communication: choice of words – sentences – tone – interaction

Step 3: What is the main function of this scene in the film?
Place the scene into the context of the film. Does it move the action forward, build suspense, present a surprising turning-point in the action, reveal a new trait in the protagonist's character, introduce a new character, or define a relationship?

Step 4: Third viewing – focus on cinematic devices
→ How do cinematic devices serve the main function of the scene?
Cinematic devices → possible functions
camera operations: field size – movements – positions – angles
visual symbols (an object stands for sth else) → to visualise an idea or message Type 1: universally understood symbols (the American flag, the cross); Type 2: symbols which take on a meaning in the context of the film, e.g. through repetition or special emphasis (close-ups)
film music/sound → to show a mood or a character's emotions, to evoke nostalgic feelings for a past era, to foreshadow an event, to build suspense, to provide transitions between scenes, etc.
montage, e.g. **flashback** → to provide background information, to recall a past event **flashforward** → to show future developments **cross-cutting** → to show links between parallel events **jump cut** → to cut out irrelevant action
other effects, e.g. **computer-generated imaging** → to create realistic images, to turn artificial figures into convincing characters, to improve images, to create locations **slow motion** → to intensify the moment, to underline effort or frustration **fast motion** → to suggest superhuman speed/power **voice-over narration** (voice speaking off-screen) → to give background information, to fill in gaps in the story, to reveal a character's thoughts, to convey the impression of a first-person or impersonal narrator

Now use your skills

Look at the first few minutes of a film – for example your favourite one. Go through the four steps described above and find out as much as possible. The note-taking sheet on the next page might help you.

1.5 Note-taking sheet: Film scene analysis

Use this sheet for note-taking when analysing a film scene. You can also use it to develop your own self-styled note-taking sheet based on the special tasks set in class or in a written test. The step-by-step approach on page 69 will help you to fill it in systematically.

Action

setting
time:

place:

plot

suspense
(unanswered questions)

Narrative techniques

Main function of the scene

Characters

appearance

body language
(face, gestures, movement)

use of language/communication

Cinematic devices

Camera operations

Visual symbols

Film music/sound

Other (special) effects

Evaluation: A Comment

1 Comment

1.1 Getting started: Types of comment

Definition !

There are three different kinds of (personal) comment:

- **"pros and cons"** comment /argumentative essay: to look at a problem from two sides
- **"support or criticism only"** comment: to express an opinion about a statement
- **"first-second-third"** comment: to give examples of, or reasons for, something

Tip !

In all comments, the way ideas are connected is very important.
This is achieved by
- the use of **connecting words.**
- the way ideas are grouped together in **paragraphs.**

Usually you are asked to express your own opinion. But you may also be expected to write "in role", that is from the perspective of someone else (see the last task in the grid below).

Always read the tasks carefully. The phrases in bold print show you which type of comment you are expected to write. Examples could be:
- Discuss whether … is **a blessing or a curse.**
  → **"pros and cons" comment**
- What **arguments** could be put forward **in favour of** … ?
  → **"support or criticism only" comment**
- What role should the computer play in school? **Give examples**.
  → **"first-second-third" comment**

Some tasks are not completely clear with regard to the type of comment. If in doubt, play it safe and choose the "pros and cons" comment. It is considered to be more objective. Examples:
- To what extent do you agree with … ?
- Assess the importance of standards in education.
- Evaluate the evidence presented in the text for the author's suggestion to …

Tip !

The task often gives you further hints, for example
- to comment on a certain aspect of the given text (→ **With regard to** the situation presented in the article, …).
- to use your results from the earlier tasks (→ **On the basis of** your findings so far …).
- to connect your comment with texts and topics from your work in class (… **referring to** different standpoints as discussed in class,/… **comparing** … with literature dealt with in class …).

Now use your skills

Decide which type of comment these tasks ask for. Underline the "signal words" in the tasks.

Task	Type of comment
Discuss advantages and disadvantages of …	"pros and cons"
In the role of a civil rights campaigner, argue against … .	✎
Which advantages make the … so fascinating for … ?	✎
Do you agree with … ? Why, why not?	✎
You are the headmaster of the school described in the text. Justify your decision to ban smoking at your school.	✎

1.2 Connectors

You will need connectors for a wide range of different functions within your text. They show the reader in what direction you are going with your next sentence(s) and therefore make it easier to understand your text. Connectors can best be learned in categories according to their functions.

a) *Match these 18 connectors with the correct category so that you have* ***three*** *alternatives in each box.*

To start with • All in all • Especially • Also • In terms of • Therefore • Admittedly • For instance • Yet • Most importantly • In short • In comparison • As opposed to • As regards • … such as • Moreover • Firstly • As a result

Useful phrases: Connectors !

Starting First of all,	people should be aware of the fact that …	**Drawing conclusions** For this reason	we have to consider that …	**Emphasising** Above all,	if we think of …
Adding In addition,	many experts point out that …	**Contrasting** In contrast to	A, B also sees the problem of …	**Indicating a topic (change)** With regard to	the global dimension, …
Summarising To sum up,	there is no doubt about it that …	**Making concessions** However,	it remains to be seen if …	**Giving examples** For example,	the danger of …

In a comment you are expected to give an opinion. When doing this, use **different phrases for variation.**

b) *Invent arguments and finish the* ***Useful phrases*** *in the box below. Read the phrases and sentences out loud to reinforce your memory.*

Useful phrases: Giving an opinion !

In my opinion/view, ______________________ should be banned.

To my mind, parents are not allowed to ______________________

I am of the opinion that everybody has a right to ______________________

I hold the view that most people are interested in ______________________

My own view of the matter/problem is that this policy is ______________________

I am sure/convinced that ______________________

It seems to me that ______________________

Personally, I firmly believe that ______________________

Useful phrases: Showing an attitude (sentence adverbs) !

Surely, everybody will be happy about ____________

Obviously, nobody expects ____________

Clearly, it is necessary that ____________

Undoubtedly, the risk of ____________ should not be underestimated.

Surprisingly, not many people know that ____________

Interestingly, experts have predicted that ____________

Strangely enough, some teenagers cannot live without ____________

Luckily, nobody expects teachers to ____________

c) *Write down all the phrases you remember (two times eight!) on a separate sheet of paper. Then focus on those you have forgotten.*

1.3 Paragraph-writing and "mini-comments"

Connectors alone are not enough to make the logical structure of your comment clear to your readers. You also have to divide your text into smaller units: paragraphs. Each paragraph develops a single argument, which means that you should start a new paragraph whenever you begin with a new idea or topic. Usually the first sentence in a paragraph is the so-called **topic sentence** which clearly states what the whole paragraph is about. The other sentences add additional information such as details and examples.

To practise paragraph-writing, work with the "mini-comments" on the next pages. A mini-comment contains only the topic sentences, i.e. only the "skeleton" of a comment. First, you will practise getting this skeleton right and then you will practise "fleshing out" the topic sentences.

Tip !

The basic structure of paragraphs is not only important for comments, but also for all other kinds of text you are required to write in your exam (except for some creative writing tasks).

Now use your skills

a) *Connect these five sentences to form a "pros and cons" mini-comment answering the following question:* "Do you agree with the author's claim that a stay in Britain is the ideal way to learn English? Why, why not?" *The connectors in bold print will help you to identify the five steps of the argument.*

- There are students, **however**, who become perfect in English without ever visiting an English-speaking country.
- In the text, the author **holds the view** that it is worth going to Britain to study English.
- **Undoubtedly**, some students make very good progress while studying in Britain, and enjoy themselves enormously.
- **All in all**, the success of a stay abroad depends very much on the individual student.
- **In my opinion,** this depends on how much money you have and how self-confident you are.

The five steps of the line of argument	Five-sentence mini-comment
referring to a statement	✎
argument in favour of the statement	✎
argument against the statement	✎
the writer's own opinion	✎
conclusion	✎

b) *In the "mini-comment" below, there are several reasons missing. Invent topic sentences and fill in the gaps. The comment deals with the following question:* "According to the survey, books still play an important role in modern society. What might be the reasons for this?"

The findings of the survey summed up in the article are clear: Most people are of the opinion that there are many reasons why books will always play a major role in modern society.

To start with, books ______

Secondly, people ______

Thirdly, and most importantly, books ______

In conclusion, books will ______

c) *Consider the answers to this question:* "For the author, competition is the key to global peace and wealth. Imagine you are an anti-globalisation activist and argue against this thesis."
There are already four topic sentences for the four main arguments below, together with notes containing additional ideas. Use these notes to turn the topic sentences into full paragraphs with several sentences.

Topic sentence 1 (Reference to the text: author's support of competition):
According to the final statement of the author, competition between individuals and nation states is the key to success. … **Notes** (phrases from the text): ambitious citizens • hard work • achieve aims • in the economy: progress and prosperity

Topic sentence 2 (Criticism of global competition):
In terms of global development, there is no doubt that the world economy can only remain prosperous through cooperation. … **Notes:** Problems: high oil prices • competition for resources • pollution • AIDS • poverty • terrorism Solutions: improve relationships • act together • close cooperation

Topic sentence 3 (Criticism of competition between individuals):
As regards the individual, people find it very hard to succeed alone these days in their professional and private lives. … **Notes:** increasing information • experts in one field • complex tasks • work in groups • private lives • focus on their own interests/aims • cause for unhappiness

Topic sentence 4 (Conclusion):
To sum up, I firmly oppose competition and regard cooperation as the main source of self-esteem and satisfaction in life. … **Notes:** strengthens independence/individuality • stronger relationships • solve future global challenges • flexible, willing to compromise • success in lives/careers

1.4 Writing a model comment

Step 1: Choose a topic and a model exam from the CD-ROM. What type of comment does the task ask for?
Step 2: Decide on a line of argument, write topic sentences and take further notes.
Step 3: Read the ***Connecting phrases*** *in the box below and highlight those you want to use in your comment. Then turn your notes into a sequence of paragraphs.*
Step 4: Ask a classmate or your teacher to correct the language. If you have written your comment on a computer, correct your mistakes and use the feedback and advice to perfect your comment into a "model" version. Share model texts with other students.

Useful phrases: Connecting phrases !

Referring to someone's statement/theory/opinion (in a text)
The author/speaker/...
- believes/states/suggests/claims that ...
- holds the view/is of the opinion that ...
- argues/suggests/demands that ...

According to the text, the problem is that ...
In recent years, there has been a debate on how to ...

Expressing your criticism (in general)
Whereas the author thinks that ... I feel very different about ...
Unlike the author, I find it hard to believe that ...
Contrary to the speaker, I am doubtful if ...
To be quite honest,
- I do not think that ...
- I cannot (fully) agree with ...
- I am not convinced by ...
- I would like to question the view that ...
- I reject the idea that ...

In my opinion/view ...
- this argument is wrong/weak/unconvincing.
- the author ignores a fact/forgets to mention sth/ is not aware of sth/focuses too much on sth/does not realise that ...

Expressing your support (in general)
The author is absolutely right in saying that ...
I do not think anyone would disagree with the author's statement that ...
The speaker has my full support when he argues that ...
In fact/As a matter of fact,
- I believe it is fully justified to say that ...
- I agree entirely with the speaker in saying that ...
- I am of exactly the same opinion as ...
- I share the view that ...

To my mind,
- this argument is very strong/powerful/convincing/plausible.
- the author presents a convincing argumentation/ discusses the topic in detail/bases his case on facts and figures.

Making concessions
To a certain extent, I can accept ...
However, we shouldn't forget that ...
Most of the arguments are hard to dismiss. Yet there are experts who ...
I agree in principle, but ...
Personally, I would not go so far as to say that ...
Although ..., we should accept/must admit that ...
In spite of all this, ...
Admittedly, ..., but ...

Your conclusion/summary
To sum up, .../In short, .../Considering all these arguments, ...
I would conclude that .../I have come to the conclusion that ...
It is safe to say that .../I would support the view that ...
My suggestion is that .../My appeal to ... is: ...

Giving arguments/reasons
One reason for my criticism/scepticism is that ...
Another/A second/A further/An additional argument I would like to present is that ...
I would also argue that ...
Another point I would like to make is that ...
The main reason, however, is that ...
The most convincing argument is that ...
That brings me neatly to my final and most important point: ...

1 Letters

1.1 Personal letters/E-mail

There are two types of letters – the **personal** and the **formal** letter. In a personal letter/e-mail, e.g. to a friend, you are basically free to choose your own language and form. However, in a course test situation it makes sense to keep the following in mind:

1. Use informal language and a conversational tone, e.g.

- *short forms*: I'm/We're/There's/They didn't
- *question tags*: …, don't you?/…, couldn't they?/…, aren't we?
- *colloquial words* e.g. Hi …/See you!/guy/fed up

2. Follow these typical phrases for each step in your letter/e-mail:

Only for print letters: Writing your address and the date (letterhead)	top right corner: [*no name!*] your address [*may also be left out*] date
Beginning your letter/ e-mail (salutation)	Dear Jennifer, …/Hi John, … [*continue with a capital letter*] Thanks (very much) for …/It was nice to hear from you. I hope you are well./I'm having a great time in … at the moment. Sorry I haven't written for so long./Sorry I haven't been in touch.
Referring to the last letter/e-mail you received	I am glad/pleased/sorry to hear that …/I couldn't believe it that …/I didn't know that …
Starting a new topic	Did I tell you that … ?/Have you heard that … ?/You'll never guess what happened to me yesterday./ Before I forget it: … By the way, …/That reminds me of … [*new paragraph for a new topic*]
Coming to the end of your letter/e-mail	That's all my news. What have you been up to?/How are things with you? How is … doing? Drop me a line when you have time./Keep in touch. I'll write again soon./I'll be in touch again as soon as possible. Give my regards/love to … Look forward to seeing you soon/to hearing from you soon.
Finishing your letter/ e-mail (closing phrase)	(With) Best wishes,/All the (very) best,/Best regards,/Love (from),/Lots of love,/See you soon,/Miss you,/Take care,/Hope to see you/hear from you soon, … Thomas [*first name only*]

Now use your skills

a) *This e-mail is rather formal in tone, language and style in some parts. Use the advice and input from above to make it more personal.*

6th April 2017

Dear Mark,

I am writing in response to your last e-mail which I was delighted to receive yesterday and read with interest. I can assure you that my family members are all in perfect health. Considering the fact that after my return to Germany I did not contact you for a longer period of time (which I now find almost inexcusable!), I am very grateful for your quick reply.

The weather here in Germany surely invites criticism because the never-ending rain and the low temperatures make outdoor activities impossible. I am sure your weather far surpasses ours in all respects. Although the forthcoming A-level examinations require an unexpectedly intensive preparation, your e-mail has found me in a confident state of mind. Are you aware of the fact that these examinations are already due to take place in the first weeks in May?

To be perfectly honest, I am still deeply worried about the challenge of writing a personal letter, a text format my English teacher has

clearly not adequately prepared me for. I am very concerned about the amount of time he spends on analysing poetry – and the only form of letter he seems to be familiar with is the letter to the editor of a quality newspaper. The polite phrases I have learned in this context appear to me slightly out of place in a personal letter like this.
Thus I am writing to request information on how to write personal letters. I hope you will find the time to write an e-mail of advice.
Thank you very much in advance for your help.
I am looking forward to hearing from you in the not too distant future.
Yours faithfully,

Sebastian Schuhmann

b) *In the role of Mark, respond to this e-mail. Prepare your e-mail by:*
- *marking the points you would like to respond to in the original e-mail,*
- *collecting some more points you would like to mention,*
- *ordering your points and notes.*

Tip !

E-mails follow the same rules as letters (except your address is normally given at the bottom of the e-mail, below your name). Usually, they are written in a very brief way. Personal e-mails can start just with the name (John,) or simply with "Hello" or "Hi!".
- **E-mails to friends use informal language as in a conversation.**
- **Popular abbreviations are: FYI (for your information), BTW (by the way), LOL (laughing out loud).**
- **Emoticons or "smileys" are also common: ;-) (joking); :-) (happy); :-((sad).**

1.2 Formal letters

In a course test, you may be asked to write a **formal letter** in which you give your opinion on something or ask somebody to do something. Use formal language (e.g. no short forms) and write in a matter-of-fact tone. Pay attention to the following conventions of a formal letter:

Writing the addresses and the date	top right corner: your address (with phone number and e-mail address), date [*but no name!*] left-hand side: name and address of the receiver [*starting on the line below the date*]
Beginning your letter (salutation)	Dear Mr/Mrs/Ms + family name, [*use Ms when you do not know if the woman is married or not*] Dear Sir/Madam, [*if you do not know the name*] Dear Sir or Madam, [*if you do not know if you are writing to a man or a woman*]
Giving the reason for your letter	First paragraph (start with a capital letter): I have been informed that you …/I would like to respond to/reply to … I am writing to ask whether …/to say that …/to comment on …
Coming to the end of your letter	I am looking forward to hearing from you soon. Thank you very much in advance for your help.
Finishing your letter (closing phrase)	Yours sincerely, [*you know the person's name*] Or: Yours faithfully, [*you do not know the person's name*] Thomas Zimmermann [*your handwritten signature; in addition often a typed one, too, especially if your handwriting is not very clear*]

A special kind of formal letter is the **letter to the editor** of a newspaper. It comments on an article, event or opinion which has recently appeared in this newspaper. In the formal letter of response on the following page you get information on how to write a letter to the editor:

16 Main Road
Ipswich
Suffolk IP3 7TG
England

8th June 2017

Thomas Zimmermann
Hammerstr. 345
48154 Münster
Germany

Dear Mr Zimmermann,
Thank you for your enquiry about how to write a **letter to the editor** of a newspaper. As a student of English, you may find the following tips and advice useful.
After writing the addresses, the date and the reference line, simply begin your letter to the editor with "Sir," (or "Madam," if you are sure the editor is a woman) and end with just your name and place of residence. Do not use "Dear …," and "Yours sincerely/faithfully".
At the beginning of your letter, state which article you are referring to. **Useful phrases** for doing this are the following:

- *In her article of 6th May 2017, "(title/headline)", the author said that …*
- *With reference to your article of 6th May 2017, "(title/headline)", I would like to …*
- *I am referring to …/With interest, I read …*

Keep in mind that a letter to the editor is meant to be printed. So make it short and to the point!
Start a new paragraph for each new idea.
Make sure that you use formal language, e.g. use "I am" instead of "I'm". Avoid complex sentences and flowery language.
Be as polite as possible, especially when expressing criticism. Please find enclosed a **list of useful phrases** at the end of this letter.
I am hoping that this advice will encourage you to write letters to the editors of English-language newspapers. Feel free to contact me at any time with further questions.

Yours sincerely,
K. Jones
Kathryn Jones

Useful phrases: Expressing your opinion politely !

After carefully studying your suggestions, I am sorry to say that …
Unfortunately, you forgot to mention that …
Please allow me to voice my criticism of your …
At this point, I do not hesitate to clearly voice my scepticism about …
In fact, I would like to express doubts about …
I would appreciate more objectivity/realism when …
I was hoping for a more impartial treatment of this subject.
With respect, I would advise you to rethink your proposals.
An option you have possibly not seriously considered is …
Undoubtedly, it might be more acceptable if you suggested …
If you had thought of different solutions, you would have gained more support …

Now use your skills

Write a letter to the editor in response to the newspaper article "'Affluenza' teen Ethan Couch (…)". (→ see p.22) *Comment on the event and always remain polite!*

2 Speeches

2.1 Getting started: Basics

In your exam you are likely not only to analyse somebody else's speech, but also to write a speech yourself. Being able to analyse something is a useful prerequisite for producing it yourself, so make sure you are familiar with analysing speeches before you continue. (→ see pp.18–21)

Tip !
to give/make a speech, talk or statement (on/about sth)
not: ~~to hold a speech~~

a) *The three tasks below do not refer to any texts in this book, but show you different kinds of tasks which you might encounter in an exam. In all three of them you are expected to write the script of a structured comment on a topic which is to be delivered to an audience on a certain occasion. Read the tasks carefully and underline keywords.*

Example 1: Both students from your school and American exchange students take part in a formal debate on whether globalisation is a positive process or not. Give the introductory **statement**, in which you critically refer to the views expressed in the given leading article.

Example 2: On an exchange visit of your class to an English school, you are invited to take part in a discussion on the topic "Can a multicultural society really work?" Your contribution is a **talk** in which you comment on the topic from a German perspective, also considering the findings of the survey described in the text.

Example 3: In a speech in front of young college students, a member of the American government responds to the critical comments on US immigration policy made in the given article. Write the script for this **speech**, referring to the principles of American immigration policy and the concept of the American Dream.

b) *There are small but notable differences between the terms* ***'speech', 'talk'*** *and* ***'statement'***.
Fill in the correct term in the definitions below. If you need help, look them up in a dictionary.

The ______________ is the longest and most formal one.

The ________________ is usually the shortest of the three text types.

The __________ may be less formal and more entertaining than the others.

c) *Answer the following questions for the three tasks above. Fill in the gaps, and be aware of what you are expected to do.*

Questions	**Tasks (above)**	**What you have to do:**
Who is speaking? If you are not the speaker: What is his/her perspective on and knowledge of the topic?	Task 1: you (as a critic of the opinion given in the text) Task 2: ✎ Task 3: a member of the US government ("you are speaking in role")	• Choose fitting (formal) language (choice of words) and keep your tone serious. • Use informal language and humour only for a special effect. • Present yourself as a confident and trustworthy person.
Who is being addressed? Is your audience described in the task? What are its expectations?	Task 1: ✎ Task 2: mostly English pupils Task 3: ✎	• Choose the right address: Ladies and gentlemen, … • Connect with the listeners at the very beginning: I really appreciate being here with you today … • Take up their expectations: I know what you expect me to do: … • Use easy rhetorical devices, e.g. contrast: Undoubtedly, this is a time of … But at the same time it is also a period of … • Ask for support and trust.

Questions	Tasks (above)	What you have to do …
… on what occasion?	Task 1: ✎ Task 2: ✎ Task 3: possibly at the college (following an invitation from the college or another organisation)	Be aware of your role and the formal character of the occasion: • Stay calm and logical. • Work with arguments and reasons. • Speak clearly and directly. • Use appropriate language.
… on what topic?	Task 1: the process of ✎ Task 2: the concept of a ✎ Task 3: ✎	• Find ideas in the text which you can use or refer to in your speech. • Note down any further ideas from class work: facts and figures, arguments, key words and phrases.
… with what intention?	Task 1: to criticise the views of the articles Task 2: to ✎ Task 3: to ✎	Think of a clear structure and a convincing line of argument. (→ see p.71 to revise the types of comment and practise ordering your arguments)

2.2 Structure

A speech has to be carefully structured in order to be effective. (→ see p.20) *In the left column of the following grid, read the ideas and advice for the three parts of every speech. In the right column, fill in appropriate phrases for the introduction, the main part and the conclusion from the* ***Useful phrases*** *box on the right.*

Useful phrases: Introduction, main part and conclusion of a speech !

- Let me conclude with the words of … who once said that …
- Ladies and gentlemen, …
- For this reason …
- I am hoping for … Thank you for listening/for your attention.
- First of all, …
- It is an honour for me to be here today at …
- All my evidence points in one direction: …
- I feel greatly honoured by your invitation.
- An additional argument for … is …
- Looking at all the facts and figures, I have to draw the conclusion that …
- As some of you might know, since my early childhood I have taken a special interest in …
- You might all remember XY who said many years ago: "…"
- This brings me to my final point: …
- What it all boils down to is the following: …
- Let us all work together to …
- We are here today to …
- For instance/for example …

The three parts – ideas and advice	Useful phrases
Introduction 1. Greet the audience politely. Thank them for the invitation. State your topic and its importance. 2. Catch your listeners' attention e.g. with … • a provocative statement or question • a surprising fact or trend • a new discovery • an eye-opening experience • an anecdote, joke or quotation 3. State your aim. (Outline the structure of your speech.)	✎
Main part Hold your listeners' attention: 1. Develop your ideas step by step, e.g. • in chronological order • from the least to the most important idea • all arguments against and then all those for an idea • alternate arguments for and against a certain idea • connect problems with solutions 2. Back up your ideas with background information. 3. Give examples to support your statements. 4. Divide your speech into clear units (paragraphs). 5. Link the parts of your speech. 6. Repeat and emphasise important ideas.	✎
Conclusion 1. Come to a convincing end, e.g. with one of the following … • a short summary • a quotation • a call for action (appeal) • a look into the future • a rhetorical question • a promise • an appeal 2. Finish your speech clearly.	✎

2.3 Rhetorical devices

Rhetorical devices may make a speech more effective. Here's a list of examples:

Identify the devices (in bold print) in the following sentences from a speech on the USA. Copy them into the column of the grid on the next page.

1. Becoming an American citizen is **like winning an Oscar**.
2. ~~There is no country which is **more generous, more accepting and more welcoming** than the United States of America~~.
3. We Americans are still the **lamp lighting** the world.
4. **Send him** back to Washington for four more years!
5. This is a question of **war and peace**.
6. ~~**Should we ignore the threat of terrorism?**~~
7. Martin Luther King once said: **"I have a dream."**
8. **We need** strength. **We need** hope. **We need** courage …

Rhetorical devices	Examples (America)
rhetorical question	*Should we ignore the threat of terrorism?*
enumeration (list of three)	*There is no country which is more generous, more accepting and more welcoming than the United States of America.*
appeal to the audience (e.g. imperatives)	✎
imagery, e.g. simile or metaphor	✎
quotations	✎
alliteration	✎
contrast (antithetical phrase)	✎
anaphora (beginning sentences in the same way)	✎

3 Newspaper articles

3.1 Newspaper comments and letters to the editor

There are many different types of newspaper articles (→ see p.23) which can become the subject of a text production/creative writing task in your exam. However, writing a newspaper comment or a letter to the editor is not too different from writing other letters or comments:

- A **newspaper comment** basically follows the rules of a personal comment (→ see pp.71–75) but do not forget to add a headline and to write in the third person.
- For how to write a **letter to the editor**, turn to the section on letters. (→ see pp.77–78)

If you are asked to write a news story, however, there are a few more things to pay attention to. Read the following pages and maybe have a look at the chapter on analysing newspaper articles again, where the structure of news stories is explained in detail. (→ see pp.22–23)

3.2 News stories

A newspaper story (or newspaper report) deals with a current event ("hot news"). Its main aim is to inform objectively about what happened. However, the way of presenting the news and the selection of details may to some extent reveal the journalist's attitude.
In any case, make sure you ...

... check the task and the text:
- What type of report are you expected to write: a (conventional) news report (facts only) or a news story (the event and the story behind it, and maybe also the writer's personal opinion)?
- What type of newspaper do you write for: a popular or a quality paper? You may, for example, be asked to turn (a part of) a quality newspaper article into one from a popular paper.
- Scan the exam text for facts to include in your article. For example, you may be asked to write a news story about the plot of a literary text.

... use the journalistic style your newspaper demands:

Writing for a ...	**popular paper**	**quality paper**
Your intention is ...	• to inform and entertain the reader!	• only to inform the reader about the event!
You would like to address a ...	• less educated readership	• more educated readership
Choose the suitable journalistic style:		
→ When presenting the event and the people, ...	• focus on "human interest" • dramatise the event by exaggeration and gossip • make the event unusual, sensational and extraordinary • personalise the event with special emphasis on the people involved • speculate on motives and further developments • offer a ready-made opinion on the event	• focus on "facts and figures" • describe objectively what happened • report what the eye-witnesses, experts, the police etc. say about the event (variety of observations and comments) • allow the reader to form his/her own opinion
→ When writing the report, use ...	• everyday language (with some colloquial or informal language) • emotional words • short sentences • questions and exclamations	• formal language • neutral words • longer and more complicated sentences

Now use your skills

a) *The article below is a fictitious report of the first meeting of Romeo and Juliet (Act I, scene 5 in Shakespeare's play), as a local newspaper might have written it. Read it carefully and decide whether it belongs to a quality or a popular paper. Underline the phrases which are most typical for the chosen journalistic style.*

Montague kisses Capulet

Will this lead to total war?

Verona. Last night a scandalous event took place at the famous Capulet's masked ball. Our reporter Mike Lennon, who managed to gain access to the party, acquired inside information and took these outrageous snapshots. Shockingly, he observed a mysterious stranger kissing Lord Capulet's attractive daughter Juliet. Was it love at first sight or a planned meeting? Also present at the gala were glamorous Paris – bachelor of the year and Juliet's future husband – and Juliet's uncontrollable cousin Tybalt.

The conflict between the Capulet and Montague families has dragged on for several generations. The people of Verona have become used to the street fighting. However, the surprise kiss at the Capulet's party last night is likely to take the family feud to a new level. The question asked by many people right now is, "Which Montague could have the courage for such a risky action?"

Fortunately, Lennon pulled some strings and uncovered the masked man's identity. When he got in touch with Juliet's nurse to obtain inside information, he learned that the stranger's name is Romeo, the son of Lord Montague! How the two were able to meet up, we don't yet know. Our editorial staff is currently on the scene and trying to get to the bottom of this story. However, one thing is certain: Romeo must have been completely out of his mind to have illegally attended the Capulet's party. Tybalt, who is well known for his aggressive behaviour and strong anti-Montague feelings, saw Romeo and almost killed him on the spot. He would have succeeded if it hadn't been for Lord Capulet who stopped him at the very last second. Luckily for Romeo, Paris was not aware of the intrusion.

The breathtaking news of this extraordinary incident is currently spreading across Verona like wildfire. People are uncertain about the safety of our streets and parks. Now that a Montague has offended the Capulet's family name and pride, the future of Verona is at risk. To be sure, the *Verona Sun* will keep its readers up to date on the scandal and the breaking news events of the day.

b) *The first paragraph (the "lead") usually answers the five Ws. Fill in this grid with examples from the fictitious article above:*

Who?	
Where?	
What?	
When?	
Why?	

c) *Scan the news story for useful language for an article in a popular paper, e.g. words and phrases for …*

Tip !
Remember: Use the past tense when describing the event!

dramatisation or speculation:	scandalous, …
comments:	Shockingly, …

d) *Rewrite the news story as it might appear in a quality paper, concentrating on the facts. As you can leave out all the dramatic details and speculations, your report can be much shorter (about 80-100 words).*

4 Interior monologues and diary entries

4.1 Interior monologues

When dealing with fictional texts, you might be asked to focus on the exploration of a **character's mind**, i.e.

- to slip into the role of one of the characters,
- to put into words what goes on in the character's head.

a) *Make sure you are familiar with the following terms. All of them refer to processes in the human mind or consciousness. Find pairs which are close in meaning. Put them into the correct boxes in the grid on the next page.*

~~memories~~ • feelings • fantasies • thoughts • emotions • ~~recollections~~ • daydreams • ideas

Past	Present		Future
memories recollections	✎	✎	✎

As these processes are **nonverbal**, an author has to '**translate**' these processes into **language** if he/she wants to show what goes on inside a character's mind. The two most common methods of doing this can be found below:

Reported thought	Interior monologue
third-person point of view mainly uses past tense	first-person point of view mainly uses present tense
Both make use of: jumping quickly from one thought to the next – exclamations – incomplete sentences – short forms – questions	

Now use your skills

b) *In the short story "Mr Mumsford" the reader gets no information about what is going on in the principal's mind. Go back to the chapter about short stories and read this story once more.* (→ see pp.29–30) *'Freeze' the story at the moment when the principal meets Bibs in the hallway.*

c) *Focus on the principal: To prepare an interior monologue you have to answer these three questions:*

- What situation is the principal in?

He is at school at night ("a little past ten" (l.9), "office" (l.10)).

- What is his personality like?

We have very little information. He ...

- What kinds of feelings, thoughts, memories etc. might be rushing through his mind at this moment?

d) *The last question is answered in the following two texts, which represent the two different methods of showing what happens in a character's mind. Read them carefully and then add a few more lines to each of them.*

The principal's thoughts as reported thought:

Was Bibs seriously threatening him? Planning to attack him with the baseball bat he was clutching? After all, there were beads of sweat on his forehead. Signs of tension and anger. This was it! The situation he had rehearsed in seminars about psychology many times. Would he be able to remain calm and act professionally? ✎

The principal's thoughts as an interior monologue:

Why is he looking at me like that, clutching a baseball bat? I've never seen that anger in his eyes before. Maybe I've never looked. He's always seemed so good-natured and docile. Steady. I must not show him I'm worried. Show him that I understand – that's what I must try to do. ✎

4.2 Diary entries

a) *A diary entry is in many ways very similar to an interior monologue. Find the three parallels and the three differences in this list on the right and complete the grid (parallels first in the first three lines):*

Interior monologue	Diary entry
personal/private/secret	
✎	
✎	
invisible and inaudible, usually not written down	✎
✎	✎
✎	✎

- first-person point of view
- main focus on the recent past
- thoughts at a certain moment
- visible, written
- ~~personal/private/secret~~
- addressed to oneself
- main focus on the present
- ~~invisible and inaudible, usually not written down~~
- statement on a page with a date

Although in a diary entry the main focus is on the past, present emotions and dreams and hopes about the future may also play a role.

b) *These nine structures are often used in diary entries. Look at the tenses and write three structures into the correct column of the grid below.*

- ~~Why did he/she not do sth in time?~~
- I wonder what he/she is doing at the moment.
- I wish sth could/would happen.
- If I had done sth, sth else might have happened.
- It's hard to accept sth.
- I dream of sth happening.
- I know/I am certain sth will happen.
- When he/she was doing sth, I felt uncomfortable.
- I bet he/she doesn't know how to do sth.

Past	Present	Future
Why did he/she not do sth in time? ✎	✎	✎

Now use your skills

c) *In the section on analysing poetry, you can find the poem "Rice will grow again".* (→ see p.40) *Read it carefully and collect information about what happened back then and what we learn about Mitch.*

Situation: ____

____

Mitch's personality: ____

____

d) *Imagine Mitch has had a nightmare in which the dead farmer plants rice shoots around his bed. Write a diary entry where he tries to cope with the dream. You may start like this, for example:*

He was there again last night, the farmer with the rice shoots. There were shoots all around my bed ...

5 Dialogues and interviews

5.1 Argumentative dialogues

In an argumentative dialogue the two participants usually give their opposing opinions on a topic. In an exam, the dialogue is partly based on the given text, so it is likely that the first opinion on the topic is to be found in the text.

The following hints are essential to writing a convincing dialogue:

Structure your dialogue: The first speaker should introduce the topic and say in general what he thinks about it. Organise your ideas in a pros-and-cons table and number them in the order in which they are best discussed in the dialogue. Clearly end your dialogue (e. g. *It's been very interesting to share our views on this topic. We should continue the discussion as soon as possible. See you soon.*).

Use spoken language, e. g. the speakers could
- give short answers (*Yes, I am./No, I'm not.*).
- use "fillers" to play for time (*Actually/As a matter of fact/To be quite honest .../What I'm trying to say is that .../Just let me get this right .../How shall I put this/ I must admit that's a good question.*).
- emphasise key statements (*In fact, I didn't quite say that. What I* did say *is that .../What I find very interesting is that .../What shocks me most is .../The point I'm trying to make is that ...).*

Act and react, e. g. the speakers could
- interrupt politely (*Just a second, .../Did I understand you correctly? .../Sorry, would you mind explaining why ...?/I'm sorry to interrupt, but ...).*
- sometimes change the subject (*What is also interesting in this context is that .../That reminds me of .../That raises another question which we should try to answer, namely ...*).
- give "turn-taking" signals, e. g. by a question tag *(..., isn't it?)*, by asking for an opinion (*How do you feel about that?*) or a pause as indicated by three dots (*Some people will surely see this very differently ...*).
- respond to what they have heard (*That's an interesting point./I must admit I haven't thought of that./That's certainly a new angle on the topic./ Do I understand you correctly here: Do you believe that ...?/You have not quite convincingly argued that .../But at this point you have forgotten to mention that ...*).

Now use your skills

a) *To prepare a dialogue on globalisation, use a pros-and-cons table for the two participants. Brainstorm ideas and complete the grid below by filling in the right-hand column.*

Participant 1: in favour of globalisation (hopes)	Participant 2: critical of globalisation (fears)
in the developing world:	in the developing world:
• new jobs	• dependence on foreign support
• rising living standards	• ✎
• less poverty	• ✎
in the industrial world:	in the industrial world:
• expanding international trade	• ✎
• new business opportunities	• ✎
• spread of freedom and democracy	• ✎
for humankind as a whole:	for humankind as a whole:
• more understanding and friendship	• ✎
• global political institutions	• ✎
• universal values	• ✎
• general prosperity	• ✎

b) *Write an argumentative dialogue on globalisation based on the notes below for what speaker A and B could say. The first few notes are already turned into complete sentences to help you get started.*

A **(refers to an article in a newspaper related to globalisation):**

Have you read today's editorial in "The Times"? It says we will all benefit from globalisation, and should learn to live with it. Selling our products worldwide, conquering new markets – sounds like a 'brave new world' of opportunities, doesn't it?

B **(points out that globalisation is a complex topic with many aspects):**

Never trust the papers, even if it is supposed to be a quality paper! Globalisation ...

A **(underlines the advantages for the developing world)**

B **(expresses criticism and fears)**

A **(describes the hopes of the industrial world)**

B **(voices disagreement and gives warnings)**

A **(the bright future of humankind as a whole)**

B **(expresses scepticism, ends the dialogue)**

5.2 Interviews

In an interview, the **interviewer** asks questions and the **interviewee** (usually an expert or celebrity) answers them. The task of the interviewer is to explore the topic and the interviewee's opinion on it through a sequence of questions (possibly pre-formulated in a questionnaire). Although sometimes asking "hard questions", he/she basically has to stay neutral and calm at all times.

Structure:

Like in an argumentative dialogue, structure is essential, so the interviewer should

- open the (public) interview with a short introduction of the topic and the interviewee (*Today's topic is ... and I've invited somebody who many people consider to be the expert in this field. Good evening, Mr/Mrs Smith!*).
- connect answers and questions (*You have argued that ... Does that also mean that ...?*).
- show flexibility by picking up interesting things said by the interviewee (*What do you mean when you say that ...?*).
- end the interview by thanking the interviewee for giving the interview (*I'm sorry to say that our time is up. Thank you for being here and sharing your views with us ...*).

Questions:

Plan an interview with a two-column table for questions and answers. Always start with the questions as they control the interview. Vary your interview with a good mix of

- short, direct questions (e. g. *How important is it to ...?/To what extent does ...?*). Avoid 'yes-/no- questions'.
- questions which you prepare with one or more sentences as "mini-statements" (e. g. *We haven't talked about ... yet. What do you think about it?*).
- fact-finding questions (e. g. *To start with, please tell us about how you became interested in ...*).
- confrontational (e. g. *Some experts criticise you for .../How would you respond to them?*) or even provocative questions (e. g. *Some people consider your attitude as leaning to the extreme right and demand your arrest ...*).
- indirect clues to certain experiences to offer the interviewee the chance to talk about certain things related to the topic (e. g. *You did some research on .../You spent some years abroad doing volunteer work in this field ...*).

Now use your skills

In the role of a reporter for a German news magazine, prepare questions for a short interview with a British politician of Pakistani origin (Mr Khan). Turn the notes into questions and then use your knowledge of British society to formulate plausible answers.

Interviewer's notes	Questions	Answers
welcome – introduction of the topic and the interviewee – Britain as a model for Germans?	Good evening, Mr Khan! Our topic today is the British experience with immigration, and what Germany can learn from it. You have lived in Britain for 30 years and have been politically involved for half that time. Some experts propose that Britain could serve as a model for Germany. What do you think about that proposal?	Britain and Germany have played very different roles in history. In spite of these differences, it makes sense to study the situation in other European countries.
Britain's history of post-war immigration? – mostly legal immigration	✎	✎
development of immigration and changing mood since 2000	✎	✎
comparison with Germany? advice to German society?	✎	✎
ending the interview	✎	✎

6 Continuing or changing prose texts

When dealing with a short story or a novel extract in a course test, you may be asked to
- rewrite a part of the text from a different point of view. (→ see p.35)
- write a different ending or to continue the story up to a new ending.

A new ending of a prose text has to continue the given text in terms of
- **action**: Logically continue the storyline up to a new, plausible ending (which may be happy/ unhappy, surprising or open). Find and take up foreshadowing hints in the text to make the continuation believable. In an additional scene, a new setting is possible, i.e. a change of place and time.
- **characterisation**: Make sure that the characters basically act "in character", but feel free to include a surprising action.
- **point of view**: Take over the narrative perspective of the prose text.
- **language**: Imitate the language of the author (in descriptions) and the characters (in dialogues).

Now use your skills

The last sentence of the short story "Mr. Mumsford" was: "Then he turned and walked down the dark corridor toward the green exit sign leading out to the playground." (→ see p.30) *Follow the principal on his way back home and describe what happens then. You can start like this, for example:*

The principal slowly crossed the playground and walked the short distance to his house beside the school library.
His wife of 23 years stood in the doorway, expecting him. There was no reproach in her calm voice. "You've been working late. I'll put your supper into the microwave."

1 Mediation

1.1 Getting started: Characteristics of a mediation task

Tip !

In its original sense, mediation means a person's attempt to end a conflict between two other people or groups. In language learning, mediation is one of the five communicative skills (in addition to writing, speaking, listening and reading).

Mediation means expressing important ideas of a spoken or written text in another language *(Sprachmittlung)*. The most common mediation task in a written exam asks you to mediate a German text (the **input text**) into English (the **target text**). Possible input texts are written texts and listening texts.

Caution! *Mediation is often mixed up with translation. Read the mixed statements about mediation and translation. Which of them belong to mediation, which to translation?*

You ...	Mediation	Translation
should follow the text word-by-word.		
are free to paraphrase.		
have to copy the style and language of the input text.		
should use vocabulary the addressee is used to.		
should leave out information if it is not important at all.		

1.2 Understanding the situation and the task

Usually, a mediation is embedded in a specific situation (or scenario/context). The situation includes information which will help you to get into the task. Read a mediation task carefully and pay attention to the following aspects:

1. the addressee: who are you writing the text for?
2. the target text: what kind of text do you have to produce?
3. your relationship with the addressee: which style of language/register do you have to use – formal or informal?
4. the purpose: what information should you focus on?

Now use your skills

a) *Read the following three tasks, underline the relevant information and fill in the boxes. The first gap has been done as an example.*

Task A	
You take part in an international school project called 'The Future of the EU'. The project explores issues of migration and integration in contemporary Europe. Each participant has been asked to contribute the example of one public figure from his/her country to the project's website. Write an article based on the essay at hand by a Turkish-German politician. Present the politician's experiences and conclusions.	Addressee: international readers (students and teachers) of the website __________ Target text: __________ Register/Style: __________ Purpose/Information needed: __________ __________ __________

Task B	
Your American e-pal thinks about studying in Germany after high school. He/She is looking for general information, individual experiences and practical advice. On the internet, you have read the report about German universities. Sum up relevant information as part of an email to your American friend.	Addressee: ____ ____ Target text: ____ Register/Style: ____ Purpose/Information needed: ____ ____ ____

Task C	
You are attending an international youth conference on "Relations and challenges in a globalised world". As a German participant you have been asked to give an opening statement. To start off, you have decided to refer to the given speech of the German chancellor. Write the beginning of your script. Outline the chancellor's views on Germany's present relationship to its allies and the impact of migration on Germany.	Addressee: ____ ____ Target text: ____ Register/Style: ____ Purpose/Information needed: ____ ____ ____

b) *In each of the three tasks A–C, there are verbs which tell you exactly the text type and topics of your mediation. Find these verbs* (Operatoren).

Task	Operator	Definition
A	*present*	give a concise account of the main points or ideas of a text clarifying culture-related aspects if necessary
B	✎	
C	✎	
A+C	✎ (+ text type)	produce a text with specific features

Tip !

Always read the mediation task carefully. Find and highlight the four pieces of information as well as the *Operatoren* verbs. It is also advisable to make a note of this essential information to refer back to when doing the task.

c) *Formulate your own mediation task based on this information. Use two* Operatoren.

Information for the task:	
Addressee:	your British online pen pal's English teacher
Situation:	he/she is planning a science fiction film night on visions of future societies – you have just read the *Spiegel Online* review of the film "Alles was wir geben mussten" – you would like to suggest the original film "Never Let Me Go" as an option for this film night.
Target text:	email
Register/Style:	formal
Purpose/Information needed:	utopian and dystopian features of the society in the film you suggest

Tip !

A mediation task mainly refers to *Anforderungsbereich I* – comprehension but also to a minor extent to *Anforderungsbereich II* – analysis.

Analysis here does not mean a formal interpretation but → selecting, ordering and presenting text information.

Your task

____
____
____
____
____
____

1.3 Skimming and scanning

Task D

Your American partner school is doing a project on Digital Lifestyles and has asked for articles about current trends in other countries to be published on the project website. You have read the following article "Vorsicht 'Smombie': …". Use the information in the text and write an article in which you present the meaning of the word 'smombie', the behaviour of German pedestrians according to recent studies and the response of the German authorities.

a) *Analyse Task D.*

Addressee: ______

Target text: ______

Register/Style: ______

Purpose/Information needed: ______

b) *Then look at the input text and*
- *state the author, source and date of publication of the text*
- *skim the text, i.e. read it quickly for its topic and function*

Author: ______

Source: ______

Date: ______

Topic/function: ______

Tip !

You can underline or highlight the relevant passages. The information on one aspect may be presented in different sections of the given text. Parts of the text may be irrelevant for the task.

c) *Read through the text. Scan it for the three aspects of* ***information needed*** *for the* ***purpose*** *of the task. Mark the relevant parts using three different colours. The first aspect has already been highlighted for you in green.*

d) *Make notes in English next to the relevant passages. Stick to the German text first, but feel free to generalise or paraphrase to prepare for a* ***concise*** *report. As an example, the notes for the first aspect have already been given in the margin.*

Meaning of the word 'smombie':

risk of carelessness → possible victim of an accident

danger in public, traffic unpredictable for drivers, cyclists and others
"smombie": smartphone + zombie (= addict)
do not pay attention to their environment

Vorsicht „Smombie": Darum sind Smartphones auch für Fußgänger ein Risiko

Ein junges Mädchen bleibt mitten auf der Straße stehen, holt ihr Handy raus, beginnt zu tippen. Erst als ein Busfahrer hupt, wird ihr klar, wo sie steht. Beobachtungen wie diese sind in Europas Großstädten keine Seltenheit, wie es in einer Studie der Dekra-Unfallforschung heißt. Jeder sechste Fußgänger ist demnach irgendwie mit seinem Handy beschäftigt. Schnell noch Mails checken, Facebook füttern, Nachrichten bei WhatsApp schreiben – die Smartphone-Generation „Kopf unten" ist nicht nur am Steuer, sondern auch zu Fuß eine Gefahr im Straßenverkehr.

[…] Das Problem: Als „Smombie" wird der Fußgänger für Autofahrer, Radfahrer und andere unberechenbar. Das Jugendwort „Smombie" - eine Kombination aus Smartphone und Zombie - beschreibt Menschen, die von der Umwelt nichts mehr mitbekommen, weil sie nur noch auf ihre Smartphone starren.

Ein Blick aufs Handy und rasch noch rüber über die Straße: Fast 14.000 Fußgänger wurden für die am Freitag veröffentlichte Studie beobachtet. Von denen, die mit den Gedanken wohl nicht auf der Straße, sondern am Handy waren, tippten die meisten einen Text ein, telefonierten oder taten sogar beides gleichzeitig. Andere trugen Ohrstöpsel oder Kopfhörer, was darauf schließen lässt, dass sie vor allem Musik hörten - und nicht den Straßenverkehr. „Telefonieren, Musikhören, die Nutzung von Apps oder auch das Tippen von Textnachrichten sorgen im Straßenverkehr für riskante Ablenkung", sagt Clemens Klinke vom Dekra-Vorstand.

Verboten ist das Ganze nicht. Während „Smombies" als Autofahrer mit einem Bußgeld von 60 Euro und einem Punkt in der Flensburger Verkehrssünderdatei rechnen müssen, werden sie als Fußgänger nicht bestraft. Eine Ordnungswidrigkeit sei das nicht, sagt Michael Schossig, Sprecher der Stuttgarter Polizei. Im Landesverkehrsministerium in Stuttgart hält man von einer Bestrafung von Fußgängern auch nichts: Die Vollstreckung sei schwierig. „Wir setzen auf Aufklärung, Vernunft und Freiwilligkeit."

[…] Der Blick nach unten ist ein globales Problem: Mit einem Augenzwinkern soll eine Universität in den USA eine „Text Lane“ (Textspur) eingerichtet haben, auf der Studenten mit Smartphone laufen sollen. Auch in China wurden schon Gehwege für Smartphone-Jünger gesehen und in Antwerpen gibt es ebenfalls eine eigene Spur für Handy-Nutzer.

Jüngere Fußgänger der „Generation Kopf unten“ nutzen die Smartphones der Studie zufolge häufiger als ältere. Mit mehr als 22 Prozent war die intensivste Nutzung in der Altersgruppe zwischen 25 und 35 Jahren zu beobachten. Laut Dekra sind 22 Prozent aller Verkehrstoten in der EU Fußgänger. Nach Angaben des Statistischen Bundesamts wird jeder zehnte Todesfall auf deutschen Straßen durch falsches Verhalten von Fußgängern verursacht.

Das Smartphone boomt und boomt: Mehr als sechs von zehn Bundesbürgern nutzen die internetfähigen Handys, wie der Branchenverband Bitkom errechnete. Das entspricht mehr als 44 Millionen Deutschen mit Smartphones. […]

Der Autoclub ACE verweist auf eine Studie, nach der Jugendliche alle siebeneinhalb Minuten auf ihr Smartphone schauen. Dieses Verhalten sei im Alltag antrainiert und lasse sich nicht einfach abstellen.

dpa, 2016 *(465 Wörter)*

e) *The first paragraph ("meaning of 'smombie'") has been written for you with the notes above. Turn your own notes on the second and third aspects into two more paragraphs for your article. Write on a separate sheet of paper and leave some space for the headline and introduction.*

The German youth word "Smombie" – short for smartphone zombie – highlights the recent trend that people who are busy on their smartphone in public have become a danger for themselves and others. Various smartphone activities distract their attention and cause unpredictable and careless behaviour, which increases the risk of traffic accidents.

f) *Task D asks you to write an article as target text. Therefore you need a headline and a short introduction for the three paragraphs. Write a suitable headline and the introduction.*

Tip !

For the headline, you have to adapt the given article's headline so that it reflects the special topic of your article.

For the introduction, use information from the task.

2 Information in context – popular types of target texts for mediation

In a mediation you present the information in a certain **context**. The context determines the **addressee** and the type of **target text**. Depending on the addressee and the target text you have to decide on the register/style (formal/informal), the structure of the text (headline, paragraphs, address), content (how familiar is your addressee with the topic/German culture?) etc. Look at the following two examples:

Name the target texts asked for in tasks A–C on pages 90–91:

A: ____________________ B: ____________________ C: ____________________

2.1 Target text: Article

For example, in exercise e) and f) above (Task D) you have already embedded information into the target text 'article'. When writing an article for teachers and students like in Task D, you use **formal style** and make up a suitable **headline** and **introduction**.

2.2 Target text: Email

When writing an email you need an **address** and a **topic in the reference line**.
Depending on your addressee you have to decide if the style of writing is **formal or informal** and how to **begin and end** your message.

Example: Task E

Your English friend's social science teacher Mr Butcher is planning a science fiction film night on visions of future societies. Having just read the *Spiegel Online* review of the film "Alles was wir geben mussten", you would like to suggest the original film "Never Let Me Go" as an option for this film night. Write an email to your friend's teacher in which you summarise the utopian and dystopian features of the society in the film as presented in the review.

Tip !

Phrases to address:
- formal: Dear, Sir/ Madam, To whom it may concern, etc.
- informal: Dear, Hi, etc.

Phrases to end:
- informal: Bye, Take care, All the best, etc.
- formal: Best/ Kind regards, Yours sincerely (if name known), Yours faithfully (if name unknown), etc.

a) *Analyse the task and fill in the gaps.*

Addressee: ______________________________

Target text: ______________________________

Register/Style: ______________________________

Purpose/Information needed: ______________________________

Tip !
Check the conventions of a formal letter if you want to write a formal email.

b) *Use the information from the task to write the beginning and ending of the email.*

To: j.butcher@btinternet.com
RE: *(reference line)* ______________________________

(form of address) ______________________________,

(introduction/reason for writing) My friend David, ______________________________

____

____

____

______________________________ [...]

(End) ______________________________

______________________________ *(your full signature)*

2.3 Target text: Script for an opening statement

When writing the **script for an opening statement**, again you need to think about how to embed the information, e.g. how to begin and end your statement.

Task F

You are attending an international youth conference on "Relations and challenges in a globalised world". As a German participant you have been asked to give an opening statement. To start off, you have decided to refer to the given speech of the German chancellor. Write the beginning of your script. Outline the chancellor's views on Germany's present relationship to its allies and the impact of migration on Germany.

Use the information from Task F to write the introduction and the ending of your opening statement. Address the audience directly at the beginning and at the end of your speech.

______________________________ *(form of address)*

(introduction/reason for speaking) ______________________________

____

____

____

____

[paragraph on Germany's relationship to its allies]
[paragraph on the impact of migration on Germany]

(end)

3 Mediation Practice I

Practise the mediation skills from chapters 1–2:

a) *Analyse the following task.*

b) *Mark relevant information in the text and take notes.*

c) *Do the mediation task on a separate sheet of paper.*

Task G	
Your friend from England wants to know what teenagers in Germany are like. Looking for reliable information, you have come across the online STERN article on the SINUS youth study. Write an email to your friend. Outline the key findings of the study and the comments of the scientists.	Addressee: ______ Target text: ______ Register/Style: ______ Purpose/Information needed: ______ ______

Teenager in Deutschland: „Hart feiern, aber gute Noten"

Rebellion war vorgestern: Teenager in Deutschland suchen der neuen Sinus-Jugendstudie zufolge den engen Schulterschluss mit der Elterngeneration. Für soziale Absicherung nähmen Teenager eine noch größere Nähe zur Welt der Erwachsenen in Kauf als die „Generation Golf" vor ihnen, interpretiert Jugendforscher Klaus Hurrelmann das Ergebnis. „Das geht schon in Richtung Überanpassung."

Hurrelmann schrieb das Vorwort zu der Untersuchung, die Sozialwissenschaftler am Dienstag in Berlin vorstellten. Überrascht hat die Forscher die Toleranz der jungen Generation – von Zuwanderung bis Religion. „Die Akzeptanz von Vielfalt nimmt zu", folgert Studienautor Marc Calmbach.

Forscher werten den ungewöhnlichen Kuschelkurs der Jugendlichen, den es so seit der Nachkriegszeit nicht mehr gab, nicht als Bequemlichkeit. Sie deuten die spürbare Sehnsucht nach Halt und Geborgenheit vielmehr als eine Reaktion auf Wirtschaftskrisen, Terrorgefahr und eine unübersichtlichere, globalisierte Welt.

Überrascht hat die Wissenschaftler der ausgeprägte Mainstream in der jungen Generation. Viele Teenager, mit und ohne Migrationserfahrung, wollen sein „wie alle". Auffällige Szene- und Subkulturen sind verschwunden. „Die" Jugend gibt es dennoch nicht: Es bleiben Gruppierungen von Konservativen über Ökos und Spaßfraktion bis hin zu Frustrierten, die sich abgehängt fühlen.

Die Sinus-Studie untersucht seit 2008 alle vier Jahre, wie die 14- bis 17-Jährigen in Deutschland „ticken". Dazu führen Jugendforscher lange Interviews mit 72 Jugendlichen zu ausgewählten Themen, dieses Mal auch zu Flucht und Asyl.

Toleranz wird im Ergebnis in fast allen Jugendmilieus groß geschrieben. Anders als in der Welt der Erwachsenen ist die Sorge vor Zuwanderung kein großes Thema, Teenager zeigten eher Mitgefühl mit Flüchtlingen. Dazu kommt ein Pragmatismus, den die Forscher der jungen Generation generell attestieren. Zuwanderung sehen viele Jugendliche nur so lange als akzeptabel an, wie die Kapazitäten für eine gelungene Integration ausreichen. Ressentiments gegen Flüchtlinge fanden sich auch - allerdings häufig in Form von Stereotypen, die Teenager vom Hörensagen kannten. Die Wissenschaftler erklären sich die Offenheit auch mit der multiethnischen Wirklichkeit, in der viele Jugendliche heute aufwachsen, vor allem in großen Städten.

Oben auf der Prioritätenliste stehen Gemeinschaft, Familie, Sicherheit und Wohlstand. Dazu kommen Freiheit, Toleranz und soziale Werte. Für die Planbarkeit von Leben und Karriere nehmen Jugendliche klassische preußische Tugenden wie Pflichterfüllung in Kauf. Was nicht heißt, dass sie auf Ich-Fixierung, Spannung, Spaß und Risiko bis zur Ekstase verzichten. „Hart feiern, aber gute Noten", lautet ein Credo.

Für Teenager gibt es kein Dasein ohne Internet und Smartphone. Leben heißt „online sein". Ohne soziale Medien drohe Ausgrenzung, lautet ein Fazit. Die bedingungslose Faszination aber beginnt zu bröckeln: Der Umgang mit neuen Medien ist mit Blick auf die Herausgabe persönlicher Daten zunehmend kritisch und selbstbestimmt. Zum ersten Mal wächst eine Minderheit, die sich der digitalen Dynamik mit dem Wunsch nach Entschleunigung zeitweise entziehen will. „Die Jugendlichen sind bestens mit Geräten ausgestattet und wunschlos glücklich", sagt Calmbach.

stern.de/DPA, 2016 *(454 Wörter)*

Your English notes:

3.1 Choosing the right register

*The mediation **Task G** asks for an **informal** email. Replace the underlined phrases on the left with the formal phrases for a different target text, e.g. for a formal report on the findings of the SINUS study.*

Formal phrases: conducted interviews • investigates • add • draw the conclusion • according to • attitudes to • characterise • interpret • raise the question

informal email	formal report
I have read a report on the internet by …	*The report with the title "…", published on …, focuses on …*
1. The study tries to find out what German teenagers think about …	1. The study ____________ German teenagers' ____________ …
2. The researchers have asked questions about …	2. Researchers have ____________ on …
3. The study says that …	3. ____________ the study, …
4. The scientists describe German teenagers as …	4. The scientists ____________ German teenagers as …
5. They also say that …	5. They ____________ that …
6. They see this behaviour as …	6. They ____________ this behaviour as …
7. They believe that …	7. They ____________ that …
8. They ask if …	8. They ____________ whether …

Tip !
Culture-related aspects are often difficult to translate. Just try to paraphrase or describe them in different words.

3.2 Explaining cultural differences

People living in other countries or continents may not understand the political or historical context of a statement relating to German history or lifestyles. Therefore *Operatoren* like "present/ sum up/outline" also ask you to briefly explain "culture-related aspects **when necessary**".

a) *Tick the box if you think the addressee needs an explanation for these four aspects of German culture.*

addressee	'Mauerfall'	'Kranken-versicherung'	'Aufwendungen für ein Universitätsstudium'	'Tatort'
your 17-year-old American friend who has never left the U.S.				
your friend's American history teacher				
your friend's sister, who studied and worked in Germany for a year				

b) *Explain the four terms in one or two sentences.*

'Mauerfall' ____________

____

'Krankenversicherung' ____________

____

'Aufwendungen für ein Universitätsstudium' ____________

____

'Tatort' ____________

____

____

4 Mediation Practice II

Practise the mediation skills from chapters 1–3:
a) *Analyse the following task.*
b) *Mark relevant information in the text and take notes.*
c) *Do the mediation task on a separate sheet of paper.*

Tip !
To prepare for the *Abitur*, do the mediation tasks of the mock exams on the CD-ROM.

Task H	
You are working as an intern for *Deutsche Welle*, the international radio and TV station featuring news from Germany. You have been asked to prepare a contribution to a podcast on "Global migration". While researching the topic, you have come across the article by Freia Peters. You decide to base your contribution on her article. Write the script. Present the reasons why young Spanish people leave their home country and what attracts them to Germany.	Addressee: ______________ Target text: ______________ Register/Style: ______________ Purpose/Information needed: ______________ ______________ ______________

„Deutschland – Europas angesagtestes Land für Arbeit"

So viele Spanier wie nie kommen nach Deutschland. Das Vertrauen in die heimische Politik haben sie verloren. Bei den Parlamentswahlen stimmen sie trotzdem ab – meist gegen die traditionellen Parteien.

Maria Dolores und Jonatan hocken [...] auf dem Land im Main-Tauber-Kreis, in einer sehr kleinen Stadt namens Creglingen. Viel zu erleben gibt es für das junge Pärchen am Wochenende hier nicht, vor allem nicht, wenn man das Nachtleben im quirligen Málaga gewohnt ist.

Aber in Creglingen haben die beiden Spanier etwas, was sie in ihrem Heimatland trotz jahrelanger Suche nicht finden konnten: einen guten Job, eine Perspektive, Aufstiegschancen. Jonatan Castro Saura, 23 Jahre, und Maria Dolores Sanchez Martinez, 27, haben im September bei der Wirthwein AG, einem mittelständischen Unternehmen für Kunststoffteile, ihre Ausbildung als Verfahrensmechaniker begonnen.

In Málaga hatte Jonatan als Koch gearbeitet, Maria Dolores an der Kasse bei McDonald's. „Im Frühjahr hörten wir dann, dass die deutsche Industrie- und Handelskammer ein Assessment-Center in Málaga veranstaltet", sagt die junge Andalusierin. „Und uns war klar, wenn wir es irgendwie schaffen, dann gehen wir nach Deutschland – das angesagteste Land in Europa, um Arbeit zu finden."

Jeder zweite Jugendliche in Spanien ist arbeitslos. Nur jeder dritte findet einen dauerhaften Job. Ein Land zwischen Verzweiflung und vager Hoffnung. Am heutigen Sonntag wählen die Spanier ein neues Parlament, und die Anteilnahme besonders der jungen Leute ist enorm. [...]

„Endlich weht ein frischer Wind", sagt Maria Dolores. „Doch selbst wenn der Wandel kommt – ich glaube nicht daran, dass sich die Dinge schnell ändern." Ihre Zukunft plant sie deshalb in Deutschland. Ihr Traum wäre es, nach der Ausbildung noch zu studieren, was ihr neuer Personalchef gern berufsbegleitend unterstützen würde. Hauptsache, sie bleibt. Er muss erfinderisch sein. Allein die Industrie- und Handelskammer in Heilbronn-Franken, Partnerregion des wirtschaftlich schwächelnden Großraums Málaga, hat 700 offene Ausbildungsplätze.

Der Fachkräftemangel hier, die Jugendarbeitslosigkeit dort, das passt zusammen. Innerhalb von vier Jahren hat sich die Zahl der Spanier, die in Deutschland eine feste Arbeit angenommen hat, fast verdoppelt von 37.021 auf 62.427 (Stand September 2015).

Nicht nur die Handwerkskammer, auch die Arbeitsagentur, die Handelskammer, die Bertelsmann-Stiftung werben in spanischen Sprachschulen sowie in den Goethe-Instituten für Arbeitskräfte. Sie locken etwa damit, dass in Deutschland 80 Prozent der Ingenieure einen unbefristeten Arbeitsvertrag haben oder das durchschnittliche Einstiegsgehalt bei 42.000 Euro liegt. Das klingt süß in den Ohren vieler Spanier – zumal es keine großen Voraussetzungen zu erfüllen gibt.

Maria Dolores und Jonatan führten Bewerbungsgespräche auf Englisch, mussten ein paar handwerkliche Übungen ausführen wie Löcher bohren und Draht biegen – und bekamen die Zusage. Im Frühsommer begannen die beiden Spanier einen Deutsch-Crashkurs, im August saßen sie im Flugzeug und betraten wenig später zum ersten Mal deutschen Boden.

Freia Peters, welt.de, 2015 *(444 Wörter)*

Your English notes:

1 Speaking Skills

1.1 Getting started: Preparing for an oral exam

Using language to communicate can be done in different ways. How much time do we spend on each skill? Look at the figures to the right and match them with the skill to which they refer.

Writing | Reading | Speaking | Listening

9% | 45% | 30% | 16%

Since oral communication plays an important role in daily life situations, more focus has been put on teaching and improving speaking skills in class. To put further emphasis on the importance of speaking skills, several federal states have made oral exams compulsory. Just as in a written exam, in an oral exam you are given the opportunity to show your knowledge about a certain topic, as well as to demonstrate your presentation skills and your ability to communicate with others.

Most oral exams combine two different formats: **presentations** and **discussions**. In the presentation part you might be required to give a short monologue or speech based on a visual **stimulus** or a text. The discussion which follows can take the form of a (controversial) dialogue, debate or a role-play with two or more participants. In both formats, you are given a limited amount of time to prepare and, later, to express yourself individually or with one or two partners.

How do you prepare?

Read the info text above again and highlight the parts that form the framework (who? what? how? time? etc.) of an oral exam.

Step 1: *Go through a Pre-Exam Checklist*

☑	**General Preparation**
	Be familiar with the framework of the exam and how you will be assessed. (→ see p.99 for Assessment Criteria)
	Inform yourself about the topic of the oral. Do some research and re-read all the texts you studied in class.
	Write down possible questions or assignments related to the topic.
	Make a mind map to organise the aspects connected with the topic.
	Make a list with terms and phrases that are important for the topic.
	Check the pronunciation of words you are not familiar with.
	Practise your pronunciation.
	Revise your visual text analysis skills. Familiarise yourself with the types of stimuli you might see on the exam. (→ see pp.56–64)
☑	**Presentations**
	Organise your material in a way that works best for you by using: mind maps, notes, outline, index cards, poster, etc.
	Break your presentation into sections: Introduction, Body, Conclusion.
	Learn presentation-specific language. (→ see pp.99–100 Useful phrases)
	Rehearse your presentation in front of an audience of friends or family.
	Watch presentations online.
☑	**Discussions**
	Look for controversial issues connected with the topics you have been studying in class. Collect arguments in favour of / rejecting these views.
	Learn words and phrases that will help you to react adequately in a discussion. (→ see p.100 Useful phrases)
	Practise with friends and fellow students. Simulate a real exam situation.
	Watch political debates and panel discussions on TV or online.

Tip !

Use index cards to practise giving a presentation.

1. Break your presentation into sections and give each one a heading.
2. Write each heading on an index card and include notes. Number the cards in the order that you want to present them.
3. Give your presentation to family or friends. Practise enough that you barely need to look at the index cards.

Tip !

Record or film your presentation keeping the time limit in mind, e.g. with your smart phone. Watch it or listen to it carefully and critically. Use the criteria to assess it.

Step 2: *Know the criteria for assessment.*

In an oral exam, you will be judged on your knowledge of the topic, language, presentation skills and social skills.

Do's and Don'ts

*Read the following **Don't** constructions and reformulate them into **Do's***

DON'T	DO
Don't speak in a monotone voice.	*Vary your intonation.*
Don't mumble or speak too softly.	______________________
Don't switch dialects, e.g. from British English to American.	______________________
Don't speak too fast or too slow.	______________________
Don't let your discussion partner do all the work.	______________________
Don't give short or overly simplistic answers.	______________________
Don't use the wrong register.	______________________
Don't be rude.	______________________
Don't let the discussion become boring.	______________________
Don't pace around nervously or avoid eye contact.	______________________

Definition

Intonation refers to the rise and fall of the voice in speech. In English, a falling intonation is very common in wh- questions, whereas rising intonation is typical of yes/no questions.

Step 3: *Learn some of the following useful phrases and practise them using the mock exams provided in the following pages.*

1.2 Useful phrases for giving presentations

The following connectors can help you to structure your presentation. Memorise as many as possible.

Match the following connectors (A–H) with the correct category (1 Beginning – 9 Conclusions). Be careful: there aren't examples for each category.

A. Let me repeat what I said earlier for instance look at
B. There is strong evidence that
C. based on these figures/facts we should
D. in spite of that, we mustn't forget that
E. as a final point I would like to
F. I'll focus on three issues
G. With regard to
H. What is all boils down to is the following

1 Beginning	2 Structuring	3 Introducing a new point
I would like to start with … Let me begin with … To start with, … First let me…	There are three points I would like to make. Firstly, … Secondly,… Then Finally,…	I would like to raise another point. What we haven't discussed yet is the question if … We should also discuss what this means for …
4 Giving evidence	**5 Giving an example**	**6 Emphasizing**
Statistics/Surveys show … Most scientists now agree that … I saw this from first-hand experience. I would like to draw your attention to the fact that …	Take …, for example . Let me give you an example of what I mean by … To illustrate this point, …	I would like to stress/ underline/emphasize that .. What I strongly believe is that …
7 Balancing	**8 Making recommendations**	**9 Conclusions**
On the one hand …, but on the other (hand) … That is certainly true, but at the same time it is obvious that …	That's why … For this reason … As a result, … The logical consequence is that … This implies that …	This brings me to the end of my presentation. To conclude/in conclusion …. And now I'll be happy to answer any questions you might have.

1.3 Useful phrases for avoiding awkward pauses

Sometimes in a class discussion you need to "play for time" to give yourself time to think. Especially in an exam situation it is important to keep up the flow of the discussion. These strategies and phrases will help you avoid an awkward silence:

Strategy	Word or Phrase	
Praise or repeat the question.	I must admit that's a tricky/clever question. I'm glad you asked me that question. So you would like to know why …? You have raised a really interesting question.	
Use fillers and say them slowly.	Well, … Actually, … Anyway, … Let me think/see, …	How can I put this? As a matter of fact, … To be quite honest, … The thing is, …
Ask for time to think.	Hang on a second. Just a moment – how can I make this clear to you? Give me a moment to think about this.	
Use a long introduction before you actually say something.	What I'm trying to say is that … The point I am trying to make is that … Just let me get this right: … First of all, what I find very important is that …	
Talk first about how other people might answer the question.	Some people might say that … You could argue that …. You could also see this very differently …. I read in the newspaper a comment by … who pointed out that …	

Now use your skills

a) *For each strategy, highlight and memorize one or two phrases which you find useful.*
b) *In pairs, collect questions which you would not like to answer and find appropriate phrases to fill time. They may be e.g. too difficult: "Why are so many countries against making trade deals?" "I must admit that's a tricky question … " too personal: "How do you feel about God?" "To be quite honest, …."*

1.4 Useful phrases for discussions

Since it is very difficult to predict the course of a discussion, it is necessary that you learn as many of the following phrases by heart so that you can react quickly. Choose one from each category (1–9) and write them on index cards that you can carry around with you all the time. Look at them whenever you have some free time.

1 Interrupting politely	2 including your conversation partner	3 expressing complete agreement
Sorry, may I interrupt you for a second … I hope you don't mind, but … Can I just jump in there?	What is your opinion about/of …? How do you feel about that? I'm interested to find out what you think about …	You are absolutely right. I totally agree with you on that point. So do I/Nor do I.
4 expressing partial agreement	**5 expressing complete disagreement**	**6 expressing partial disagreement**
You're right up to a point. Maybe that's true. I've got to admit that …	I'm afraid I totally disagree with you. That is definitely not the case. I'm 100% certain of that.	It's not as simple as that. I find that hard to believe. Are you sure?
7 defending yourself	**8 returning to the original subject**	**9 ending a discussion**
That is not what I said. I'm afraid you got that wrong. You're distorting what I actually said.	Let's get back to the point … As I was saying, … But we are digressing …	We'll just have to agree to disagree on that point. I can understand you better now even though I don't completely agree. We have heard some interesting points/ new ideas …

2 Mock exams

On the following pages you will find material for mock exams. (→ For more information about analysing visuals, see pp. 56–64)

2.1 Climate change and globalisation

Task 1: Presentation

Describe and analyse the cartoon for your partner. Evaluate its message.

Partner A

Partner B

Task 2: Discussion

Starting with the messages of your two cartoons, enter into a discussion about the advantages and disadvantages of living in a globalised world. Draw a personal conclusion explaining the general development and how you see your own future.

2.2 Environment

Task 1: Presentation

Describe and analyse the photograph for your partner. Evaluate its message.

Partner A

Partner B

Task 2: Discussion

Starting with the messages of your photographs, enter into a discussion about the impact of consumerism on people and the environment. Draw a personal conclusion explaining the general development and how you see your own future.

2.3 American dreams and nightmares

Task 1: Presentation

Describe and analyse the cartoon for your partner. Evaluate its message.

Partner A

The American Nightmare

Partner B

Task 2: Discussion

Starting with the messages of your two cartoons, discuss the problems presented by each visual.

2.4 Gun control

Task 1: Presentation

Describe and analyse the photograph for your partner. Evaluate its effect on the viewer.

Partner A

Partner B

Task 2: Discussion

Discuss the problems presented by each photograph.

2.5 Artificial intelligence

Imagine you are invited to take part in a panel discussion at your school on the topic "AI – blessing or curse?" You have found the cartoon below and you think it makes an interesting comment on the topic.

Task 1: Presentation

Describe and analyse the cartoon for your partners.

Partner A

"Is it harassment if I ask the new guy to make espresso?"

Partner B

Partner C

Task 2: Discussion

a) *Discuss with your partners whether:*
- *you agree with the messages of the cartoons*
- *one of them would be particularly suitable for a handout to prepare people for the discussion*
- *you have any first-hand experience with AI*

b) *Picture the consequences the rise of AI might have for the world in 2050.*

1 Language workshop

1.1 Getting started: Evaluate yourself!

Grammar can be quite a bother – but it doesn't have to be! Many students just handle it the wrong way. There might be some areas of grammar you are not quite sure of and therefore you make mistakes here. That's frustrating of course and you feel that grammar is your personal never-ending story. But there are also sure to be fields of grammar you are very good at and which you don't need to practise intensely any more.

Therefore, when approaching grammar it is a good idea to find out one's personal strengths and weaknesses in order to practise properly.

Tip !

Make a list with the most important grammar topics: tenses, if-clauses, adverbs .... Then look at your exams and count your mistakes. Add the number to the list and you will get an impression of your needs.

Exercise 1

Have a look at some of your homework or tests that have been corrected by your teacher. Categorise your mistakes and thereby find out your strong and weak areas in grammar.

tenses → very often

definite/indefinite article → often

adverbs → sometimes

Knowing your strengths and weaknesses, you can now decide which parts of the language workshop you should do intensely and which ones you could do faster or even leave out.

1.2 Style

The following task will help you to improve your writing style when writing formal texts. First, read the examples of participle constructions shortening the sentences.

Present participle (active meaning):
Opening the book, he began to read (instead of: When he opened ...). **Having finished** reading the book, he felt well prepared. (instead of: After he had finished ...)

Past participle (passive meaning):
Asked by the judge, the suspect denied any self-interest (instead of: When the suspect was asked by the judge ...). **Having been sentenced** to a fine of $1000, the convict was shocked (instead of: The convict, who was sentenced to ...).

Exercise 1

Shorten the sentences by replacing the subordinate sentences (underlined) with participle constructions (=using the ing-form of the verbs).

1. <u>After the author had entered the room</u>, he put his mobile phone on the desk next to the entrance.
2. The author, <u>who was welcomed kindly by the host</u>, introduced himself to the audience.
3. The author, <u>who sat in front of the audience</u>, read from his latest novel.
4. <u>After the author had finished the reading</u>, he prepared to leave but he could not find his mobile phone.
5. <u>While the author was talking to his biggest female fan</u>, he noticed his mobile phone in her bag.
6. The author, <u>who had been robbed by his fan</u>, felt outraged.
7. Since this event the author feels ambiguous <u>when he talks to enthusiastic fans</u>.

1.3 Comma

Exercise 1
Explain the differences in meaning between the following two sentences from Truss's bestselling book.

"A woman, without her man, is nothing. – A woman: without her, man is nothing."

Eats, Shoots & Leaves – The Zero Tolerance Approach to Punctuation, by L. Truss, London: Profile Books, 2003: p.9.

___

___

___

Exercise 2: Differences between English and German usage
Find the punctuation mistakes in these sentences, deleting or inserting commas. Remember that in English the comma often marks a pause in speaking.

1. I believe, that this is a convincing argument.
2. Most readers will find it difficult, to follow the author's line of arguments.
3. With these arguments the writer tries, to persuade the reader, that her views are reasonable.

Tip !
Punctuation follows rules. When doing the exercises, try to remember the rules which you follow and compare them with the **Definition box** at the bottom of this page.

Exercise 3: Commas in coordinate and complex sentences
Insert commas in these sentences where necessary.

1. The critics shouldn't call this a happy ending or their understanding of this term is different from mine.
2. This text is worth discussing because it deals with a serious social problem.
3. Although the author mentions a number of reasons for his opinion I am not convinced that he is right.

Exercise 4: Commas in sentences with defining and non-defining relative clauses
Insert commas in these sentences where necessary.

1. My mother who is over sixty has a new car.
2. All that glitters is not gold.
3. John whose birthday will be soon might join our literary society.
4. The book you are reading is mine.
5. See l.43 which I also quoted at the beginning of my essay for more details.
6. The book that we are dealing with in class at the moment expresses similar ideas.

Exercise 5: Commas in sentences with particles, adverbs or adverbial phrases and participles
Insert commas in these sentences where necessary.

1. I can of course only deal with the most obvious rhetorical devices employed in this speech.
2. To my mind this is a fascinating film.
3. Strictly speaking this comparison is misleading.
4. To summarise the important points the text contains these useful suggestions to solve the problem: … .
5. However none of the film reviews meets with my approval.
6. Having dealt with the positive aspects I will now turn to the negative features.
7. She agreed too. – She went to university however.

Definition !
Defining relative clauses contain information which is relevant for the meaning of the complete sentence.
Non-defining relative clauses contain additional information which is not closely linked with the contents of the main clause and may be left out without having an effect on the meaning of the main clause.

Examples:

1) *The boy (that) you saw yesterday is coming to the party.* (**Defining** relative clause; without it the sentence doesn't make sense.) → **no comma**
2) *My sister Jane, whom you saw last night, is coming to the party.* (**Non-defining** relative clause; it contains an additional piece of information.) → **comma**

Definition !
a) Do not use a comma before a that-clause or an infinitive in English texts.
b) The comma usually separates main clauses, especially long ones, and subordinate clauses with when, as, after, until, because, although, etc. when they are placed before the main clause.
c) Commas separate non-defining relative clauses from main clauses. Commas are not used for defining relative clauses.
d) Commas are often used to separate particles, adverbs or adverbial phrases and participles from a sentence to which they apply.

Definition !

The apostrophe is used to show that words have been shortened or that something or someone belongs to something or someone (the possessive genitive).

1.4 Apostrophe

Examples of correct usage
1. It's not true – It isn't true; She shouldn't have used irony. – She should've avoided irony.
2. My nieces' bikes; Peter's sister; Today's special (offer); The crashed plane's voice recorder

Exercise 1
Read the following examples which have apostrophes in wrong places or have none although they should have one. If possible, describe the mistakes.

1. *Childrens' books → *children's books (The books are for 'children' and not for one child only; so the apostrophe follows the plural form of the noun.)*	**6. *Next weeks' programme**
2. *Delicious pizza's	**7. *The Smith's villa**
3. *Good food at it's best	**8. *Tonites show**
4. *Its too late	**9. *the USAs role**
5. *Ladie's clothing	**10. *Egypts tourist industry**

1.5 Spelling

Exercise 1
Look at the pairs and cross out the words spelt incorrectly.

beautiful • ~~beautifull~~	english • English
cannot • can not	f.ex. • e.g. (for example)
catastrophy • catastrophe	interprete • interpret
devide • divide	ll.10–15 • l.10–15
disaster • desaster	metaphor • metapher
	pronounciation • pronunciation

Exercise 2
What is wrong with these verbs? Find the correct form and spelling.

adaptate • commentate • interpretate

____

____

____

1.6 Word meanings

Exercise 1: Difficult pairs
The following words are often confused because they look similar and have similar or related meanings. Insert the correct word in the gaps.

1. politics • policy

The government's economic policy__________ meets with severe criticism from the opposition.

Barack Obama is the most prominent 21st-century figure in US ______________.

2. economic • economical

In her speech the minister pointed out ways of overcoming the ______________ crisis.

Though a millionaire, Desmond was very ______________ in all areas of life. He never bought expensive clothes.

3. critic • critical • criticism

A good ______________ will always quote convincing evidence for his views.

One should not be too ______________ of the student because she is new at this college.

The minister refuses to accept any ______________.

4. logic • logical

I don't quite see the ______________ of your suggestion.

The author draws ______________ conclusions from the evidence which he quotes.

5. think • mean

Honestly, I really ______________ it.

'Will John come?' – 'I ______________ so.'

Exercise 2: False friends

a) *Some words look and sound similar in English and German, but differ in meaning. These so-called 'false friends' may cause confusion and misunderstandings. Replace the underlined words with words which fit.*

1. Lady Macbeth is a resolute and <u>self-conscious</u> person until after King Duncan's murder.
   self-confident
2. My brother is very <u>sensible</u> and gets mad when people criticise him. ______________
3. The talk was about the <u>actual</u> political situation of the country and not about past times.
   ____
4. I'm sorry for being late. I <u>overheard</u> my alarm clock. ______________

b) *Define the meanings of the underlined words in the above sentences.*

self-conscious = shy

____

____

____

1.7 Nouns and adjectives

> **Tip !**
> Singular nouns may sometimes be followed by a plural predicate or may allow a singular and plural predicate. On the other hand, some nouns look plural, but are followed by singular predicates.

Exercise 1: Singular and plural of nouns
Insert the verbs in brackets in the tense stated. Decide also whether there are nouns which may have both a singular and plural predicate.

1. The contents of the novel __make__ (*present*/make) high demands on the reader.
2. The audience ________ (*past*/be) fascinated by the high standard of the performance.
3. The Thompson family ________ (*going-to future*/spend) three months in Spain this summer.
4. Mathematics ________ (*present*/be) a subject that only few students enjoy.
5. The majority of people ________ (*present*/want) a change in tax laws.
6. Further news ________ (*present*/be) not available at present.
7. Most people ________ (*present*/tend) to be fed up with fundamentalism.
8. The police ________ (*present*/be) investigating the three murder cases.
9. The USA ________ (*simple past*/be) the only world power after the collapse of the Soviet Union.
10. The new government's politics ________ (*present*/meet) with disapproval from the opposition.
11. Statistics ________ (*present*/suggest) that the government will be re-elected.

Exercise 2: The definite and the indefinite articles with nouns
The underlined noun phrases in the following sentences all have an article. Cross it out if it violates rules of grammar.

> **Tip !**
> Rules concerning the question whether you may or must not use 'the' or 'a/an' with abstract and collective nouns will be found in your grammar. Memorising examples may help.
> English and German usage in this field differs considerably. Look at your answers again and translate the sentences into German to become aware of the differences.

1. ~~The~~ literature is an excellent medium to educate ~~the~~ people.
2. The literature available in the library helped me to find convincing arguments.
3. The contemporary literature must deal with topical issues.
4. The history shows that tyrants cannot feel safe even if they live behind thick walls.
5. Since the Middle Ages the English history has been the story of gradual steps towards the modern democracy.
6. The history of the 19th century is dominated by the Industrial Revolution.
7. Although we tried, we did not get a satisfactory information.
8. The information which we received at the help desk was very detailed.
9. The society decided to change the rules for the membership.
10. The society cannot expect the solution of all social problems from the government.

Exercise 3: Nouns and adjectives with prepositions
Write down the prepositions which may follow these nouns and adjectives behind the words. In some cases more than one preposition may be used. Afterwards check your answers with the help of a dictionary.

1. good __at__	8. knowledge ______
2. dislike ______	9. preference ______
3. experienced ______	10. sign ______
4. fascinated ______	11. symbol ______
5. characteristic ______	12. typical ______
6. information ______	13. view ______
7. interested ______	

Exercise 4: The plural of adjectives used as nouns
What are the English translations of these plural adjectives and nouns?

die Afroamerikaner → African-Americans (avoid Afro-...)	die Gerechten (as used in the Bible) →
die Amerikaner →	die Grünen (as used in politics) →
die Armen →	
die Engländer →	die Schwarzen Südafrikas →

1.8 Verbs and adverbs

Exercise 1: Verbs with prepositions
Look at the following list of verbs and underline those which must not be followed by a preposition.
Then write down one or more prepositions behind the other verbs.

1. agree to, with, on	8. describe ________
2. comment ________	9. discuss ________
3. complain ________	10. look ________
4. consider ________	11. refer ________
5. consist ________	12. suggest ________
6. deal ________	13. think ________
7. decide ________	14. write ________

Exercise 2: The passive voice
Turn the following sentences into the passive, paying attention to the rules of word order.

1. The Shakespeare Company staged two productions of *Macbeth* last season.
2. They had collected the keys from the lost property office.
3. A pedestrian helped the blind man across the street.
4. The landlord himself showed us around the castle.
5. The ministry is supporting this project.
6. The speaker handed out copies of the text to the audience.
7. The teacher will present a model interpretation of the poem to the class.

____
____
____
____
____
____
____

Exercise 3: Verbs and adverbs
Point out the differences in meaning between these pairs of sentences.

1. He tried <u>hard</u>. – He <u>hardly</u> tried.
2. The arguments are <u>most</u> convincing. – His arguments are <u>mostly</u> convincing.
3. The man looked <u>furious</u>. – The man looked around <u>furiously</u>.

____
____
____
____

1.9 Words in context: Phrases and collocations

Exercise 1
The following phrases and sentences contain typical mistakes of collocation. Correct them.

1. *have luck → be lucky, but: have good/bad luck	8. *an easy structure →
2. *make an experience/experiences →	9. *I am strongly disappointed by the author's suggestions. →
3. *give a conclusion →	10. *The text is separated into four parts. →
4. *make difficulties →	11. *The action plays in a castle. →
5. *a heavy problem →	12. *The story takes place in Verona./*The story is placed in the Middle Ages. →
6. *a hot discussion →	13. *The audience is brought to tears. →
7. *big importance →	

1.10 Sentences

Exercise 1: Word order
Correct these sentences by changing the word order.

1. * I brushed up my English last month in London a lot.
2. * Hollywood has turned successfully an average story into a great film again.
3. * I at this point must summarise my criticism.
4. * Hispanics will be in the foreseeable future no longer a minority.
5. * The author fails to explain to her readers the situation.

1. I brushed up my English a lot ...

1.11 Conditional sentences

Often students have difficulties expressing conditions with the help of *if*-clauses correctly. English has three basic types of condition:

Definition !

Type I
Open condition
Example: *If you work harder, you will pass the exam.*
If a condition is fulfilled, something will/may/must/etc. happen.
Tenses: **if-clause:** present; **main clause:** future, modal verb, imperative

Type II
Imaginary or hypothetical condition
Example: *If you worked harder, you would pass the exam.*
If a condition was fulfilled, something would/might/etc. happen.
Tenses: **if-clause:** past; **main clause:** conditional I (would/should/might + infinitive)

Type III
Impossible or unreal condition
Example: *If you had worked harder, you would have passed the exam.*
If a condition had been fulfilled, something would/might/etc. have happened.
Tenses: **if-clause:** past perfect (had + past participle);
main clause: conditional II (would have/should have/might have + past participle)

Exercise 1
Decide whether these examples are type I, II or III conditions.

1. If the audience had known what they would see, they would not have bought tickets for the show. ______
2. If the team showed more courage, they might stand a chance of winning. ______
3. The visitors can't come unless it stops raining. ______

Exercise 2
Complete these sentences and define the type of condition.

1. If we had enough money, ______ Type II
2. If you don't agree, ______ Type ______
3. If it wasn't so urgent, ______ Type ______
4. ______ if I understand the message of the text correctly. Type ______

1.12 Tenses

Exercise 1: The simple form and the progressive form
Rewrite the sentences, inserting the correct forms for the verbs in parentheses.

1. * The author (to give) a detailed description of the heroine's character.
2. * The writer (to mention) incidents which (to complete) the picture.
3. *At the beginning of the text the author (to ask) the questions which he will try to answer.
4. *As we (to discuss) a similar topic in class at present, I (can/to give) a detailed answer.

______
______
______
______
______
______
______

Tip !
When you speak or write about texts, you generally use the simple form of the present tense.

Exercise 2: The past tense and the present perfect
The past tense and the present perfect are frequently confused. Insert the correct tense forms.

1. My son has cut the lawn so that the barbecue is not at risk. [cut • has cut]
2. My son ______ the lawn yesterday before it [cut • has cut] ______ raining. [started • has started]
3. I ______ two performances of the play up to now. [saw • have seen]
4. I ______ two performances of the play last month. [saw • have seen]
5. I ______ another two books by the author recently. [read • have read]
6. It isn't long ago that I ______ similar short stories. [read • have read]

Exercise 3: The present perfect with for *and* since
The prepositions for *and* since *are frequently confused when used with the present perfect. Fill in* for *or* since *in the gaps.*

1. I haven't read a book for months.
2. I haven't read a book ______ last month.
3. I have been taught English ______ eight years now.

4. I have learnt English ______________________ I started primary school.
5. As you have been practising ______________________ a long time now, you will pass tomorrow's test.
6. I have been waiting for my driving license ______________________ I was three years old.

1.13 Summarising tests

At the end of this chapter, you are invited to do these final tests. Find and correct the mistakes.

Exercise 1
What is wrong in these sentences? If possible, give the rule which has been broken.

1. *This view can nobody tolerate.

1. Nobody can tolerate this view. (word order)

2. *The text is separated in four parts.

____

3. *In these lines it stands, that Britain should reform their education system.

____

4. *A great number of nations loose their cultural identity as the consequence of the globalisation.

____

5. *English and german christmas customs are still very other because centuries old traditions.

____

6. *I mean, that this text which came out 2017 tries to manipulate the reader, because the arguments in line 25 till 35 are not logic, when you carefully look on them.

____

Exercise 2
Here is an excerpt from a summary of Golding's Lord of the Flies, *which needs to be revised.*

1. *The underlined words and phrases of this text are marked as wrong. Correct the mistakes.*
2. *The tense forms of the verbs in italics also meet with criticism. Correct them where necessary.*
3. *There are no commas in the text anywhere. Put commas in so that the reader can understand the sentences better.*

Ralph <u>*choses*</u> Jack and Simon <u>for to go</u> on an expedition with him because he *wants* to explore the island. After the boys *have walked* along the beach <u>some time</u> they <u>*get the idea*</u> to climb a mountain. They *thought* this *were* the <u>most easiest</u> way to find out if they *are* on an island or not. They *found* the mountain difficult to climb, but after a while they *have reached* the top and *have* a good view <u>above</u> the place. The boys *can* see <u>now</u> that it *is* an island over and over <u>couvered</u> with jungle and on the one side <u>in the near of</u> the beach a big rock, which *looked* like a fort, <u>*comes* out</u> of the water. On their way back the kids *found* a piglet caught in the dense bushes and shrubs. Jack *takes* his <u>knive</u> and *says* that he *wants* to kill the animal but suddenly he <u>*stops* to kill</u> it and it *escapes*. He <u>*excuses*</u> this <u>in saying</u> that he only *wanted* to look for the right place to kill the piglet so it *was able* to escape. After this <u>happening</u> the boys *go* back to their platform.

Enough of grammar for now – but remember: to keep fit you need constant practice!